The
Necessity
of
Being

Also by Joseph Chiari

The Aesthetics of Modernism
Anthology of French Poetry
Britain and France, the Unruly Twins
Columbus's Isle
Contemporary French Poetry
Corsica, the Scented Isle
The Eagle of Prometheus (*poems*)
France and the War
France and the Problems of Peace
The French Contemporary Theatre
Impressions of People and Literature
Landmarks of Contemporary Drama
Lights in the Distance (*poems*)
Mary Stuart (*verse play*)
Paradoxes (*poems*)
The Poetic Drama of Paul Claudel
Realism and Imagination
Reflections on the Theatre (*translation*)
Religion and Modern Society
Symbolisme—from Poe to Mallarmé
White Temple by the Sea (*poems*)
T. S. Eliot, Poet and Dramatist

The
Necessity
of
Being

Joseph Chiari

Docteur ès Lettres

Paul Elek London

Published in Great Britain 1973 by
Elek Books Ltd
54–58 Caledonian Road   London N1 9RN

ISBN 0 236 15471 0

Printed in Great Britain by
Clarke, Doble & Brendon Ltd
Plymouth

Contents

One could at the same time assume, as Bohr has suggested, that our knowledge of a cell being alive may be complementary to the complete knowledge of its molecular structure. Since a complete knowledge of this structure could possibly be achieved only by operations that destroy the life of the cell, it is logically possible that life precludes the complete determination of its underlying physico-chemical structure.

One may hope that the combined effort of experiment in the high energy region and of mathematical analysis will some day lead to a complete understanding of the unity of matter. The term 'complete understanding' would mean that the forms of matter in the sense of Aristotelian philosophy would appear as results, as solutions of a closed mathematical scheme representing the natural laws for matter.

WERNER HEISENBERG : *Physics and Philosophy,* 1959

Author's Foreword

The main themes of this book have long been part of my mental preoccupations and writings. Professor Monod's book *Chance and Necessity*, a book which can be argued about but not ignored, compelled their crystallization into book form. His extrapolations from his no doubt remarkable work in the field of biology to that of philosophy have led him to adopt conclusions and beliefs which, as he disarmingly says himself, are such that they can only be upheld or opposed with the utmost earnestness.

Finding myself unable to subscribe to the view that 'only pure chance—absolute, blind freedom—is the source of every novelty and creation in the biosphere', I have, at the outset, endeavoured to show that the concept of chance used here is a metaphysical concept and, as such, rationally untenable. On the other hand, chance as an operational concept applied to possible mutations in biology or atomic particles' behaviour in physics, or to the probability of the occurrence of certain events, is a perfectly workable concept, pertaining to the domain of the calculus of probabilities.

I am all too aware that, from Aristotle to Hume, Cournot, Keynes, Russell, Kneal, Popper, Ayer and others, the study of probabilities and statistics is a specialized study implying a knowledge of logic, mathematics and mechanics which I do not possess. I therefore hope that specialists in this field will understand why I have avoided any critique of their studies, and confined myself to the examination of chance as a metaphysical concept, which plays a dominant role in Professor Monod's book, despite the fact that he sometimes uses chance as an operational concept.

Introduction

Until very recently philosophy has constantly tried to deal with questions about the origins and the why of things, the meaning and purpose of life and of the universe, and about the ultimate nature of goodness, truth and being. Our age, dominated by positivism, pragmatism, linguistic analysis, empiricism and Marxism (an empirico-positivistic ideology combining scientific evolutionism and Christian theology), has no great interest in the philosophic vision which attempts to reach beyond the range of experience, sense-data and materialism. Both Christian and Heideggerian existentialism are deeply concerned with the fundamental question of being, but Sartrian existentialism is not, and its interests are more and more psychological and sociological.

The light of reason, which, from Plato to Descartes, Kant and Hegel, could embrace the varying relationships of the finite and the infinite, the interplay of the one upon the other, and the flux of becoming which either mirrored eternity through Time or turned Time into eternity or the absolute, is now mostly bounded by the curtain of the senses, and is no longer allowed to try to grasp and describe the glimmers which rise from the deep sea whence we emerged and to which we return. The appearance, the data of the senses, the verifiable, are all that matters. The noumenal world and the absolute are generally dismissed as abstractions or as meaningless notions, and this in spite of the fact that Kant is the acme of rationalism and that Hegel has not only closed the cycle of rationalistic idealism which links Hellenistic thought to Cartesian idealism and to the philosophy of mind, but is also the founder of modern phenomenology, which through Husserl, Merleau-Ponty and Sartre plays an important part in modern thought.

Modern thought cannot, of course, be reduced to positivism, empiricism, Marxism or atheism; this would be a gross over-simplification of the mental structure of our age. It would mean ignoring the importance and range of Christian thought. For most Christians immanence and transcendence are realities which have not been abolished either by those who are afraid to use the word 'God' or those who think that Christ as a figure of music-hall or of musicals can make religion acceptable to jaded minds. Besides that, there is still the immanentism and transcendentalism of Hinduism, Judaism and Islam, and there are hundreds of millions of people who feel very strongly that though religion is not and will never be a question of know-ledge, it is something deeply rational, and as such it is believed in.

In spite of the prevailing belief in experience, in the principle of verifiability, most people still believe in Hamlet's words to Horatio: 'There are more things in heaven and earth, Horatio, than are dreamt of in your philosophy.' They also believe that the world's major problems, like wars, pollution, starvation or the gap that separates the rich from the poor and the oppressed from the oppressors, can only be solved in a world dominated by true socialism—religious or humanistic—which, in contra-distinction to that of today's so-called socialist states, will respect the individual and make of his inalienable rights to free-dom the basis, for himself and for others, of the political, social and economic structure of the state.

This will not come about quickly or without severe pains and suffering, but it will certainly come, for, as Hegel put it: 'God is cunning. He lets men do as they please with their particular passions and interests, but the result is the accom-plishment not of their plans but of His, and these differ decidedly from the ends primarily sought by those whom He employs.' Seen from afar, from the moon for instance, or from timelessness, the jagged coasts of the earth, or the progress of man and history from beginning to end, look like a straight line. The being which informs the world accomplishes itself through it, and everything that is, is what it is in its essence, part of Being. The actualization of being produces the illusion that a given end is progressively realized and revealed, while in fact the revelation consists really in the getting rid of such an illusion, for the end merely reveals what is already there, idealized in Being. The world is what it is, and the sooner we realize that, the sooner we shall shed vain and useless attempts to make streams flow upwards or the earth revolve from East to West. The problem is not to change the laws of the universe, but to know what they are, and by knowing them to be free, by being an expression or an emanation of this true knowledge and not a negation of it. Our worldly errors, our world-embracing evil and suffering, are, alas, part of the dialectic of truth, for it is only by negating its opposite that an idea, part of Being, can reveal its truth.

Modern positivists and empiricists may very well claim that statements about the ultimate nature of things are beyond experience, not verifiable and therefore meaningless. Yet man, whatever the historical time or place he lived in, has always had a mind which, whatever its working methods, may be fed and comforted or discomforted by the senses, but is reducible neither to matter, nor to an epiphenomenon of matter, nor of course to a plasmic entity with a life and finality of its own. Man's mind is an extraordinary combination of animated, purposeful matter and being or energy, which contains in itself coded connections between the finite and the infinite and is therefore capable of knowing what truly is, and of increasing, through this individual knowledge, the knowledge which is both the source and finality of life.

Positivists and empiricists maintain that philosophy cannot tell us what things in themselves are, and that it can only analyse various theories and systems and point out the basic elements of these theories and systems and the way they work. Philosophy, according to them, can only clarify propositions and constructions that men make, but it is not its business to ask questions which cannot be dealt with through analysis, or answered—if they are related to matter—by positive science. The key to this attitude lies in the last sentence of Wittgenstein's *Tractatus Logico-Philosophicus*: 'What we cannot speak about we must pass over in silence.' Pragmatists are looked upon as psychologists in disguise, Marxists as sociologists and myth-makers, and existentialists as pure subjectivists whose notion of uncaused, unchanging, unaccountable freedom is simply nothingness. If one adds to these notions the one that not only God but man also is dead, one has an idea of the complexities and the limitations of certain contemporary philosophical attitudes, which, of course, should not be taken to represent the whole range of contemporary thought. In spite of their apparent ascendancy, due in part to the fact that the beliefs that they express are readily grasped by the mass-media and by a public which finds irreverence and iconoclasm easier to adopt and more comforting than the terror of unanswered questions or the Angst of Pascal or Kierkegaard, it would be unwarranted to believe that our age is totally dominated by anti-metaphysical aspects of thought.

No age is ever the neat pattern of forces and counter-forces which later historians and philosophers make it appear to be. It is always a kaleidoscope in which some seem to exercise more pre-eminence than others, but they are never as neatly compartmentalized, categorized and ordered as the human mind which examines them from a distant vantage-point in time and space sees them and assesses them. Every individual mind imposes its pattern upon the philosophical or historical landscape which it observes, and while the subject is part of that landscape, he is apt to think that the currents that buffet him are the most important, if not the only ones at work in his time. Yet life, and everything pertaining to mind and matter, is synchronic; it is only diachronic at the level of the individual, finite being, looked upon as a manifestation of Being, that is to say as a combination of finitude and awareness of infinity.

Ideas do not succeed one another like scientific discoveries. They are always, in varying forms and strength, part of the mind of historical man, and they are never, like scientific discoveries, replaced by new ones. They go on living, unadulterated, or assimilated and transformed into new syntheses of varying degrees of strength and importance according to the time and place from which they are viewed. They are therefore directly related to the society to which they belong, whose situation they express through individual and collective minds, and they modify it and are modified by it.

Society is a whole, and history itself is also a whole, and as a manifestation of life, it is—in spite of its dark patches, its moments of madness, its evil, its apparent or partial irrationality—rational, because it cannot be otherwise. If God or Being did not write straight with crooked characters, if both being and non-being were not part of the becoming which separates one from the other, there would only be total non-being. To become is both to be and not to be, and that is why life on earth cannot be perfection; it can only be a continuous interplay of good and bad, being and non-being, though in the end Being will prevail, for becoming has no other aim except to return to Being.

Whatever the prophets of doom or of apocalypse may think, the calamities and destructions which men cause are part of human time. Judged by human standards of morality, they are no doubt despair-laden and heart-breaking, but seen as part of the becoming of Being, they are the necessary non-being which has to be separated from being. Some people think that the marvels of science are such that some day perhaps computers will take the place of human brains, or that men will one day make life. This day will never come, for computers, however complicated and evolved they may be, will always be made by men, but life will never be made by men, since it has already been made once, and men are part of it. Therefore it can only be re-made out of already existing, human-made or -organized materials, and in ways which will not ontologically impinge upon life itself, because the relationship between the finite and the infinite cannot be altered by the finite which only is and only knows itself and others as part of the self-awareness of the infinite.

From the Hellenic world to our time, man has been pursuing this type of knowledge, which also coincides with absolute freedom, and both these aspects of man's most constant quest imply the existence, throughout the whole life of mankind, of a metaphysical and practical order which has always equated true freedom with the transcendental or the noumenal. The noumenal freedom of Kant, the freedom of Hegel who said: 'Man is most free when he knows himself to be determined by the absolute idea throughout,' the uncaused freedom of Sartre, all rejoin the Christian and Islamic notion that the individual is most free when his will coincides with that of the absolute which is both Being and non-Being, and which is also the world of pure ideas of Plato. There are certain ideas and beliefs which are part of the life of mankind, and though their formulations may vary with historical time, their essential content remains unchanged.

I

Chance

The true rationalism must always transcend itself by recurrence to the concrete in search of inspiration. A self-satisfied rationalism is in effect a form of anti-rationalism. It means an arbitrary halt at a particular set of abstractions.

A. N. WHITEHEAD : *Science and the Modern World*

Nowadays the word 'God' can hardly be spoken without provoking raised eyebrows and sneers. Even theologians have shorn Him of some of His attributes and replaced them with all kinds of subterfuges and a less awe-inspiring terminology. Nietzsche, at the end of the last century, boldly certified God as dead. I shall not comment on this paranoic genius who could not tolerate any equal, and least of all the notion of vassalage, nor shall I attempt to prove that he was wrong, and that the patient is still very much alive. There are enough contenders already at work in this field, and God, Who is older than the human animal, is not easily put to death by well-wishers, ill-wishers, doubters or budding candidates for His privileged position. I have no doubt that the multitudinous forms which He has assumed throughout the ages will have given His imagination enough scope to devise a new one to fit the sophistry and sensualism of twentieth-century man. After all, long-haired or short-haired, wearing jeans or prancing in Adam's garb, twentieth-century man is still man, with ape-like desires, love of drugs and dreams, and an irrepressible longing for mysteries which no scientist can solve or replace by so-called objective scientific truths.

There are indeed scientific truths, but they are only objective within the necessity of mathematics, and that is a ques-

B

tion to which I will return later. For the moment, let us concede to science-minded, science-loving questers and doubters the fact that huge changes have indeed taken place, and that though twentieth-century man is still the same biped as before, he certainly lives in surroundings which nineteenth-century man would hardly recognize, and which seem to alter at a bewildering speed. These changes have often enough been praised, denigrated or, at any rate, enumerated, and there is no need to repeat them once more. The froth and foam which floats on the stream of life may look different, yet the stream is still the same, and the forked animals which strut on its banks are still the same; there is no ground, or at least no serious ground, to suggest apocalyptic visions of a new and totally incomprehensible world in which man no longer knows what to expect, and where to turn for light and direction. It seems to me more useful to offer an analysis of the facts as they are, and, in spite of the prophets of doom, the facts rationally examined point to the conclusion that our fate is neither better nor worse than it has ever been, and that we can adapt ourselves to it, cope with it, and make it possible for creation to go on towards its self-determined finality, which can no more be deflected than the weight of one man could tilt or affect the equilibrium of the earth.

Creation is neither a random birth, nor a random growth, and the order to which it pertains will not be altered by the wailings of the absurdists or the fantasies of scientists who look upon it as the accidental result of a vast throw of the dice by the fairy hand of chance! What is chance?—the unpredictable, the unforeseen, the indeterminable, and consequently the indescribable? Is it an absolute or a relative notion? If it is an absolute, that is to say, if the ens of chance is all-embracing, applying to all things, at all times, if every move, every aspect of creation is always unforeseeable, unexpected, totally free to be anything, how does such a concept of chance connect and work with a fully recognized determinism? If it is relative, that is to say, if it applies to certain aspects, forms or movements of life only, if it is fractional, how does this essential unpredictability fit in with predictability and determinism? What is, in fáct, this so-called unpredictability which cannot, by its nature, be defined, yet which always ends in conforming perfectly with predictability and determinism? How could one dream of reconciling two such absolutely incommensurate concepts, for they are mutually exclusive, and they can be reconciled only by accepting the notion that what we call unpredictability might very well be temporary ignorance, and also by not confusing infinite virtualities with existential actualizations. One may dream of these virtualities, but one only knows their actualizations, and though one may posit virtualities as unpredictable, the only things the mind truly knows, measures and assesses are actualizations. Virtualities, might have beens, chance, as operational concepts, belong to the same domain of the calculus of probabilities, but not to the domain of the absolute which would make of chance the basis of life and human actions.

There are, no doubt, all sorts of events enshrouded in the future, and therefore unknown to man. There are also mysterious happenings in the universe which cannot be explained or codified, and there is the great revelation which seems to have unsettled so many minds, the famous Heisenberg principle of indeterminacy—that the position, the momentum and the velocity of an electron cannot be accurately known, because its mass is so infinitesimally small that any presence disturbs it and renders its behaviour unpredictable, although this unpredictability does not affect the atom, the molecule, the cell or the body to which it belongs. It is very likely that one day the laws of this apparent unpredictability will be discovered. Meanwhile, some of the greatest minds of our times, like Einstein and Niels Bohr, have remained unperturbed by this unpredictability, and there is no doubt that whatever its precise effect on our knowledge of the behaviour of electrons and mesons in the world of physics or even in the world of neurophysiology, there is not the slightest reason to subscribe to the belief that total unpredictability, total freedom, total randomness, could be self-caused. If they were not so, they would not be free; on the other hand, if they were self-caused, absolute freedom would be an ens, part of the essence of being which would also be, by definition, unpredictable, gratuitous, anarchic and unnecessary. This is an intractable notion, and it seems more likely that our temporary ignorance could very well be the only explanation of our attempt to believe that from chance and unpredictability, order and determinism could ever emerge. This is obviously not possible, yet this is what those who, mostly for ethical reasons, are instinctively averse from the notion of determinism and finality, which they reject by describing them as subjectivism, vitalism, animism, etc., fail to concede. Yet it must be conceded that, though some very small particles seem to organize themselves by chance, these chance organizations are reproduced practically without fail in every molecule and cell. Therefore from a 'chance-born' sequence of electrons and mesons comes a perfectly deterministic order in molecular and organic life. From chance determinism is born! Such a hybrid concept cannot be satisfactorily explained or accounted for, if one defines rigorously and precisely what one means by chance.

If one means by chance the unforeseeable, the uncaused, unintegrated, irrational, absolutely contingent aspect of life, then this concept is totally irreconcilable with any possible order. If one confines the concept of chance to a moment in time, such as that of the birth of creation, then one would have to explain how a vast number of absolutely unconnected, totally neutral elements or particles could come together and organize themselves into molecules and cells and, later on, into integrated organisms. By 'neutral' I mean entirely lacking in any complementary properties, appetitions or affinities, which could influence or direct their behaviour, for if they possessed such properties, they would necessarily be orientated towards certain unions with other elements complementary to them. If such neutral conditions did not obtain, then these primal particles would not be entirely free from compulsions, causality, finality, and therefore they could not be the prerequisite instruments of chance or hazard. Anything which exists has properties of some kind, to say nothing of the property which makes it exist, for if it were not so, it would not be. How could it be explained how particles of matter could have come into existence, how they could have passed from virtuality to actualization, unless it were that the very virtualities from which they originated had some appetitions for existence? These virtualities could not be absolutely neutral, for perfect neutrality, which could only be non-being, could only be perfectly static, and could not engender existence. Therefore perfect hazard or chance cannot be considered a logically possible notion.

The fact that there is existence proves that the notion of chance is not an absolute, but a purely subjective, relative notion, entertained according to individual needs, knowledge and beliefs. The most fervent apologists of chance, the opponents of order and finality in life and creation, talk of chance operating within evolution, within the context of DNA, of genes bearing instructions which are duly received and duly carried out. They acknowledge therefore a finality which has nothing to do with vitalism or animism, but is simply the basic property of life, the capacity to individuate itself and to maintain its individuations until the exhaustion of the process through decay, death, disintegration and reabsorption in the cycle of creation. The immanentism of life does not imply any deliberate intervention of transcendence, working for a determined, fixed finality. To look upon this problem in such a light is like holding the idea of God as a kind of bearded Moses sitting up in the clouds. It is raising aunt sallies for the easy task of knocking them down. The finality of life is not external but in itself, in the structure and organization of its component elements, and this excludes chance.

Chance cannot be caused; it can only be self-caused; if it were caused by causes external to itself, it would not be chance, but a manifestation of a causally determined order. Chance must in fact be absolute freedom, and as such it rejoins the concept of the noumenal freedom of Kant. If chance, or noumenal freedom, is what causes itself, it is difficult to reduce its manifestation to one single instance, but it is even more difficult to believe that it can cause itself repeatedly. If chance has manifested itself once, there is no reason why it should not manifest itself again, and if it does, there is no reason to believe that self-caused chance is not part of order. And besides, there is the vital point that if chance is self-caused, its self-causations must have been caused by some force which causes them to cause themselves, and so on and so on, so that this kind of argument can only be met by accepting the straightforward proposition that the self-causations of chance or of noumenal freedom must have in themselves appetitions, qualities or orientations which make it possible for their component elements to agglomerate into causes which cause chance or freedom.

Faced with such conclusions, Kant easily understood the impossible situation in which he was enclosed by his dualism involving a noumenal world to which, according to him, freedom belongs and a phenomenal world in which man and freedom operate. He was in fact confronted with the intractable antinomy that freedom, the expression of the noumenal, manifests itself through being, which is perfectly ordered. So he ended in shifting his position from the notion of freedom as pure being to freedom as being for good, or for the moral categorical imperative. He expressed his view on this point in *Opus Postumum*, in these words: 'There is in man a good principle, the voice of the categorical imperative; there is in it no evil principle, for that would be contradictory; but man is subject to the attraction of the senses.' Thus freedom ceases to be a noumenal self-caused notion, to become the result of the perfect accord of man's behaviour with the categorical imperative, or the Law, the first principle of which is 'to act as if the principle of one's actions were, by one's own will, to be erected into a universal law of nature.' The Law which man must obey is founded on speculative reason.

This is the very crux of the problem of being, which cannot be dealt with on the purely empirical plane. Man's existence, part of nature, does not quite coincide with nature. He goes beyond it, through mind, which is so intricately connected with nature as to be its heuristic spirit. Man, being a rational being, that is to say a being in whom practical and speculative reason—the reason which connects him with the transcendental—are one, is a metaphysical being. Again, in the same *Opus Postumum*, Kant sums up this point: 'There is in man an active, supra-sensorial principle, which, free from nature and worldly causality, determines the phenomenon called freedom . . . Man in the world belongs to the knowledge of the world, but man, conscious of his duty in the world, is not a phenomenon, but a noumenon, not a thing, but a person.' And he concludes with these words: 'Metaphysics is the science of the boundaries of human reason.'

For Augustine or Spinoza, knowledge of the self is knowledge of, or through, the informing substance. For Kant, who rejected Descartes' priority of the *cogito* over existence, but nevertheless retained his dualism, man's true being is freedom, or being for good or for the Law. To get out of this dualism, a dualism which does not seem to worry some modern scientists who uphold both quantum physics and classical physics, he posits man as a rational being endowed with free will, which works for reason, and by working for reason chooses freedom which realizes itself in nature and in history, and tends towards the establishment of the universal state. Morality, for Kant, can accomplish itself only through a progress which goes as far as the infinite, and requires the separate existence of a personality living indefinitely, therefore immortal. To believe in God's transcendence is not a leap into the unknown, but a way of living an autonomous and spiritual morality, which is no more synonymous with culture than thought is synonymous with knowledge. The common equation of knowledge—the notion being generally confined to experimental knowledge—with thought is one of the main reasons for the fragmentation of our age. Man is rational in the domain of pure as well as practical reason, and it is his rationality which is the cause and the basis of culture. Therefore, culture is no more opposed to nature than practical reason can, in the end, be opposed to pure reason.

If, instead of talking of some unresolved aspects of experimentalism in terms of hazard or chance, one talked of the infinite (at least from the human point of view) possibilities and virtualities from which existence proceeds, the problem would be different. It would lead straight to the only possible approach to this question, which is the approach through the possible meaning of, and the reasons for, being. This is a question which has tormented and agitated man's mind probably since he has been able to think. Countless attempts to answer it have been made, and many answers, though none likely to submit to the principle of verifiability, have been given by some of the greatest minds mankind has produced. It would be idle and fruitless to attempt a critique of the various metaphysical theories which have been put forward. There have been many such critiques which could not be surpassed or equalled. I am thinking of A. E. Taylor, of Whitehead's comments on Plato, Russell's on Leibnitz, N. Kemp-Smith on Kant, W. Kaufman and Findlay on Hegel, etc. I shall attempt only to put forward an explanation of the question formulated above as a twentieth-century, post-Heideggerian and, I should also say, post-Wittgensteinian man, and to say something in answer to the question : why being instead of non-being ?

2

The Rationality of Being

We can no more apprehend God than we can hope to know the exact origins and cause of creation. We can only speculate about them and try to see how far our speculations and hypotheses can be justified by rational judgment or experience, if not by verifiable mathematical or perceptual evidence. Irrespective of the views of some devotees of scientism, what most philosophers and great scientists do is to begin with imagination, with hypotheses, and with intuitive apprehensions of the truth. Plato, Newton, Einstein and other great scientists did not proceed otherwise. No human being is mathematically, mechanically objective. Man is always animated by beliefs, intuitions, imagination, which give him glimpses of the discoveries he endeavours to make. There is no more chance than there is random grace; 'the spirit bloweth where it listeth'. Pasteur and Fleming were not ignorant shepherds who suddenly made their discoveries while washing their hands in a mountain stream; they were scientists with ideas and imaginations searching for and intent upon finding new ways of dealing with disease. Of course they only knew exactly what they were looking for once they had found it and named it. It is just the same for the poet, who only knows the poem he wanted to write once he has fully written it. Yet he had the urge to do so, the receptivity and the vision to spur him on in his discovery of the truth. Truth is only known once it is found, and not before, and truth, as Hegel said, always comes in its due time, just at the moment when it is right and ready to be accepted.

The need for the absolute, for the transcendental, is as old as man and is inherent in man, as Leibnitz put it. The Egyptians, the Chaldeans, the Hittites, the Greeks, the Mayans, the Christians and others, have all hungered for the absolute, which is part of man's evolution and growth. 'You would not look for me, if you had not already found me,' says Christian doctrine. The search for perfection and the absolute is part of mankind, it is a thirst which no atheistic pronouncement can quench or dispose of. The dream of human perfection will never be completed, for if it were, matter would be turned into spirit, and finitude into infinity. This does not mean that man sees creation as an immense game of chess with a chess master pushing every piece in turn towards its appointed end. Men, endowed with imagination, dreaming of perfection, move about towards their only appointed end which is death, according to their own inner lights, psychological make-up, social possibilities and conditions, towards a future which they make, which reveals itself to them, but which certainly leaves no room for chance or hazard in the exact sense of these two words. Even the supporters of this notion have to concede this point. This is what Professor Monod says in *Chance and Necessity*: 'But if in this sense, every primary structure of protein appears to us as the pure product of random choice at every stage, among the twenty available residua, on the other hand, and in a sense which is just as significant as the former, it must be acknowledged that this actual sequence has not in any way been synthesized at random, since this same order is reproduced, practically without error, in all the molecules of the protein which is being discussed.'[1] He goes on to say: 'However, there is and there will remain in science a Platonist element which could not be taken from it without ruining it.'[2] Having stated that 'there is no mechanism by which a protein could be modified . . . except through an alteration of the instructions which are part of the DNA,' Professor Monod continues: 'No mechanism could be conceived of through which any instruction or information could be transferred to the DNA,' and he concludes with these words: 'The whole system consequently is intensely conservative, closed upon itself, and absolutely incapable of receiving any information whatever from the outside world. As one can see, this system, owing to its properties, its microscopic clock-work functioning which establishes between the DNA and protein, and also between organism and environment, one-way relationships, defies any attempt at "dialectical" description. It is basically a Cartesian and not a Hegelian system: the cell is truly a machine.'[3]*

Further, Professor Monod says: 'It is evident that the part played by end-controlled performances in the orientation of selection increases in importance with the level of organization, that is to say with the autonomy of the organism in relation to the environment . . .'[4] The term 'end-controlled' translates the neologism 'téléonomique' used by Professor Monod, who seems to be putting a very old and well-established notion into new garb. Finally here is a quotation which shows how difficult it is to get rid of the notion of necessity in creation: 'The *a priori* probability that out of all the possible events in the universe, a particular one should take place, is near zero.† Nevertheless the universe exists; some particular events, whose probability of coming into existence (before they actually did) was infinitesimally small, do happen. At the present moment, we have the right neither to assert nor to deny that life may have appeared only once on earth and that, consequently, before it appeared its chances of appearing were practically nil. This idea is not only unpleasant for biologists as men of science; it conflicts with our human tendency to believe that every actualized thing in the universe was necessary from the beginning of time.'[5]

The probabilistic nature of the unpredictable reactions of some minor particles of matter, under observation, has been

* All passages I quote from Le Hasard et la Nécessité (1970) are in my own translation, and not from the English edition of 1972. For convenience I refer to the work by its English title.

† The probability of an event which has happened only once cannot be assessed, neither can its meaning be fully discussed.

up to a point scientifically tested, and has led to the Heisenberg principle which has a relativistic validity. But this principle is in itself unverifiable, for to verify it would require an observer observing the observer who observes the unpredictable behaviour of the electrons. This observer would have to be entirely neutral, that is to say, have not to exercise any influence whatsoever on the observer observing the behaviour of the electrons. In order that this could be so, this observer would have to belong to an entirely different magnetic field or be of a completely different nature. He could, of course, be God, entirely withdrawn from any possible influence upon, and spiritual or material relationship with, the observer of the thing observed. This is, all in all, an impossibility, and the value of the Heisenberg principle is, by its very nature, relativistic and not absolute. It is true in the domain of probabilities, but it necessarily leaves a margin of unknown in the domain of the behaviour of the electrons when they are not observed, and this slight margin of unknown could, with equanimity, be made to testify in favour of those who believe that unobserved electrons behave according to the rules of classical physics. The chance or hazard of Democritus is purely mechanistic. It is the Fatum of the Parcae of ancient Greek mythology, who exercised their unaccountable and unpredictable power even on the gods, who were part of the laws and necessity of the universe.

The probabilistic possibilities of life coming or not coming to earth have not been tested, and can never be tested, and this for various reasons. First, we do not know, and we shall never know, the exact conditions which obtained in the course of the slow transition from chemical chaos to the first molecular aggregation. We can only try to retrace our steps backwards from our present time, through our own particular knowledge, mental and affective structures and beliefs, towards conditions which we have to interpret through thought which is not coeval with them and is not commensurate with them. Therefore the assertion that the probabilities of the coming of life to earth were so small as to be due to chance, is merely an *a posteriori* assertion without any scientific basis, since there is no possibility of verification or repetition. If we say that the probabilities of life existing in any one of the millions of solar systems in the millions of galaxies which people the universe are infinitesimally small, we indulge in a gratuitous assertion, for we cannot know the conditions obtaining in these various systems, any more than we can know the conditions obtaining on earth two or three thousand million years ago, when what is called life began to emerge. If we say that out of all the possibilities which obtained at that moment, the probabilities that a particular one should emerge are practically non-existent, and that therefore life is a unique phenomenon, we are merely making a statement of belief, not a scientific statement. We cannot know the range of probabilities and of possible events until they have been actualized. Actualization tells us what the possibilities which have been actualized were, but does not tell us and cannot tell us anything about those which have not been actualized. All we can infer is that the actualizing potential and possibilities of those which did not become actualized were insufficient for actualization; and the possibilities which have become actualized must not only have had in themselves enough existential potentialities to become actualized, but they must also have possessed the necessary appetitions and affinities which enabled them to join with other possibilities or virtualities, to reach actualization.

If we say that the probabilities of the actualization of certain possibilities were so small as to be the result of chance, then the obvious question is: what is chance, and how does it work, since it is the agent of an action? And the answer to this question, as we have already seen, is that chance has to be self-caused and to become an ens, the ens of existence—something which is a contradiction in terms. The proposition that possibilities were realized by chance rests on a basic contradiction between the verb 'to be' (were), which indicates existence, and a causal agent which is by definition non-existent, since if this agent were an existent, it ought to be definable and it ought to

be able to become the subject of the verb 'to be'. Whether the
word 'chance' is used as the subject of the verb which expresses
the action in question, or as a state in which the action takes
place, the difficulty is the same. In both cases, the agent of the
action, or the agent which makes possible the action, is unknown, unpredictable and undefinable; it has therefore no being, it is in fact non-being. The vague sociological or linguistic
definitions of the word 'chance' as a conventional concept are
not applicable on the plane of metaphysics on which this problem is being discussed, the plane of the birth of concepts and
not that of the use of ready-made concepts. On this plane the
concept of chance has to be tested at the level of being and
non-being, and therefore as a possible absolute; and here we see
at once that the concept of the coming of life to earth being due
to chance is an untenable concept, for if one accepts it,
chance—non-being—becomes the cause of being—a meaningless proposition which leads straight to Leibnitz's question:
'Why is there being rather than nothing?'

Whether being and true reality reside, as in Plato, in the idea
and not in their appearance, or whether being and reality
reside, by means of forms, in particular things, as Aristotle
suggests, the essence of being is, in both cases, to be represented, or to be given an existential appearance. The essence
of being is existence, ex-sistere, differentiation, separation from,
presence; continuation and maintenance of what is, up to its
perfection. The Aristotelian transition from idea to form informing being, and from idea to actualization, is the basis of the
Christian determination of Being as being, differentiated from
Being as idea. The notion of Being as being has moved away
from Greek thought, which in this respect has close analogies
with Eastern thought, and has become the hallmark and ener-
gizing force or entelechy of Western thought. But in both
aspects of thought the essence of Being is to be, whether to be
as idea, or as being in action; being, therefore, could not not be,
and its causation or ens, derived from pure Being through
forms, remains part of its actualization and connects it with,

and orientates it towards, the perfection of the *Summum ens*, from which it has issued.

A final and important point concerning quantum physics, which is somehow at the root of the notion that chance could be made responsible for the origins of life, or for that matter for the so-called 'big bang' which set the universe going, is that all the observations of quantum physics are made with instruments which result from and entirely conform to the laws and structures of classical physics. It was in fact the logic and unfolding of these very laws which led to the observation that, at the microscopic level of small massless particles, matter does not quite conform to the laws of classical physics. As far as this small field of physics is concerned, one therefore moves from the domain of objects which conform to structures and laws, which is the normal domain of science, to that of events. These events are by definition unpredictable, not reproduceable at will, and if one refuses to pass from purely observational truth to inferential truth, they are irreconcilable both with the notion of life as structure and with the notion of the study of their origins through the laws and structures of classical physics.

If one accepted the notion of chance as the cause of the origins of life, one could not explain how this notion of unpredictability, which is basic to quantum physics, should also have been the origin of classical physics. One would thus be reduced to the dilemma that life based on chance developed according to law and order, or that the notion of law and order was imposed upon life and took over from chance at the start. This is obviously an unsolvable dilemma, for chance subdued by a force which represents law and order is no longer chance, but merely a verbal notion. If, on the other hand, one accepts chance as the cause of the origin of life, one is driven to the strange paradox that the whole pyramid of the cosmic system, which is an intricate pattern of structures and recognizable mathematical and geometrical laws, somehow rests on the pinhead of chance and total unpredictability.

How could one maintain that one could reach the notion of original chance through physical laws and knowledge, which are essentially rationalistic and therefore, according to their essential nature, ought to have been born from an event which, though it could for the time being be claimed to be unique, is not and cannot by definition be irrational and due to chance, for if it were so, the roads which lead back to it ought to be *ipso facto* inextricable and undefinable? Would it not be more rational to avoid trying to prove, in the name of reason, that the very foundations of reason are irrational and rest on the unpredictability of chance? Should one not be aware of the contradictory nature of the attempt to prove rationally the irrational, or chance to be the basis of reason? Should one not be aware of the fact that extrapolation from the microscopic field of quantum physics to the macroscopic field of classical physics makes of the notion of event the basis of science, and that science thus becomes merely the technological observation of the operations and events of life, and ceases to be part of the perennial and that human vision which has been able to perceive the various relationships between the structures, changes and laws of the vast universe, and the structures, changes and laws of the various molecules and entities which form life at all levels? Heraclitus, Plato, Newton, Einstein, have all relied upon this same principle of intricate, indestructible relationships and structures which make of the universe a whole. And whether time and space are looked upon as separate, Newtonian entities, or are reunited into one single, Einsteinian continuum of subjective variance, which philosophically echoes the Bergsonian notion of duration, Heisenberg himself, the founder of quantum physics, has seen with the vision of the great scientist that he is that microscopic unpredictability does not disturb in any way the order of classical physics.

'We have no reason to think,' says J. D. Bernal in *The Origin of Life* (1967), 'that we are unique. Life may and indeed must have occurred in other parts of the universe, particularly in parts of stellar planetary systems similar to our own, of which thousands may exist in the visible universe.'[6] He says else-where in the same book: 'Harrison Brown's calculations already referred to indicate that there are some thousand visible stars that are each capable of carrying planetary systems with, on the average, two planets within the life zone!'[7] Life is therefore not a question of chance or accidents, but a question of facts and laws of nature which, whether they conform with the laws of numbers or with those of indefinable causality, are inherently part of matter, and in fact make matter what it is, for matter is energy, and therefore animated and chemically related to all its manifestations in the vast and timeless universe. 'Life must have had from the start either a source of free energy in itself or must have been able to take in free energy from out-side.'[8] Professor Bernal gives an admirably concentrated defini-tion of life which conforms perfectly with Christian philosophic realism and therefore could have satisfied Teilhard de Chardin, Maritain and all those whose view of matter as being informed with energy or essence can easily be reconciled with the modern scientific equation of matter with energy. 'Life,' he says, 'is a partial, continuous, progressive, multiform and conditionally interactive, self-realization of the potentialities of atomic elec-tron states.'[9] Here is a definition which reconciles immanence ('continuous') with transcendence ('potentialities'). Then he con-cludes with the words: 'There is no such thing as the origin of life. Life is originating all the time—it is a continual pro-cess of interaction between successively self-generating entities which contain elements both of necessity and of his-tory. Beginning at the beginning, it is a by-product of cosmic self-generation, of creating energy sources in the building of stars and planets.'[10]

As for chance, J. D. Bernal and his fellow scientists like P. B. Medawar, J. S. Huxley or J. B. S. Haldane leave no room for it as far as the origin of life is concerned. Bernal's view is that the theory which now states that the first living molecule came about by accident through a chance concurrence of atoms is the old Democritan picture in a new style and far less convincing

C

than the original.[11] Then he goes on to say : 'Haldane finds, for instance, that a happening of a particular sequence in a nucleotide chain requires the simultaneous occurrence of 10^{17} trials, for which there is neither space nor time enough in the whole history of the Earth . . . In any case, all arguments based on chance, apart from their insufficient logical basis, are intrinsically pointless, though they are often advanced in an apparent attempt to prove that life cannot have originated by itself at all.'[12]

The universe, or nature, inexhaustibly rich and prodigal of its infinite vitality, produces and wastes an immeasurable number of potentialities which come more or less near the threshold of actualization, or, as Aristotelian philosophy would have described it, according to the amount of form they have in themselves, or according to what would now be called their chemical components. Those which become actualized do not do so by chance; they do so on account of the laws which govern their behaviour and the attributes of their component elements. 'Not only, as Darwin proposed, are all organisms genetically related but, also, the very molecules out of which they are built are based on the patterns of the original small abiogenic molecules that were found in the primitive soup or even—and this seems most likely—on those of polymers that these molecules gave rise to in the second stage where the critical process of molecular replication first appeared.'[13]

J. Z. Young, in his book *An Introduction to the Study of Man* (1971), asks the question : 'Do the laws that control the matter of the universe contain factors, besides the known laws of physics, which dictated the necessity for life to begin (and presumably also to evolve)?'[14] And he answers thus : 'The view that it is possible to understand the origin and subsequent course of life by the operation of what may be called well-tried physical laws is therefore the only one that can be fully submitted to rational examination.'[15]

As for the role of chance in the origin of life, Young, like J. D. Bernal, quotes approvingly Haldane's conclusions, and adds: 'Dixon and Webb (1958), in a similar discussion, calculate that even if the earth had been wholly made of amino-acids and these rearranged themselves at random ten times a second there would have been little chance of forming one molecule of the simple protein insulin.'[16] Finally, concerning the question of whether life could have occurred or could occur in other parts of the universe he says: 'This raises the further controversial question of the possible presence of bacteria and other forms of life on meteorites. The compounds found in carbonaceous meteorites are similar to those formed by synthetic processes from ammonia and other gases as described above. This suggests that such early stages of biopoiesis were not confined to the earth. Indeed, there is reason on statistical grounds to think that the conditions necessary for life must occur not infrequently in planetary systems throughout the universe.'[17]

However distasteful the notion may be to some libertarians, they have on the whole to concede that Being and being could only be necessary. Whatever is, obviously has in itself enough possibilities for being. Either Being is necessary or it cannot be accounted for. Why Being instead of non-Being? That is the question, and it is no use answering that one does not know, for that is a well-known truism which will not stop the beatings of the questing mind, seeking to find a possible answer to the most heart-rending riddle of mankind. We know that the question cannot be answered, for finite being cannot encompass Being, and therefore man will not know the answer until he no longer feels the need to ask the question, that is to say when he has returned to the heart of Being. The great fact confronting us is that Being is, therefore there must be reasons and causes for it, and these reasons and causes cannot but be—are bound to be—part of Being itself; they must be its finality and its essence. Being can only be because it has to be, if not it would not be, therefore Being and everything pertaining to it are necessary, that is to say the chance, the virtualities, of Being had necessarily to be greater than the chance, possibilities or virtualities of not being. The essence of Being must be to be, just as Logos, which is also necessity or *ratio*, is the mediating essence between God and matter or creation, and the reason for individuation and incarnation, which are therefore as necessary as God or Being itself. The essence of being is to exist through becoming in creation and time, so as to return to pure Being, perfected and eternalized through becoming.

Evil, or rather what is called evil—a notion entirely shorn of metaphysical connotations—and suffering, are parts of individuated being, and unknown to Being, for the only knowledge which Being can possess is the self-knowledge of the whole, which embraces the virtualities of good and evil, being and non-being. It is the same with the existent being, whose only knowledge is also self-knowledge, though fragmented and sectional; for whether the existent being knows another being, a tree, or scientific truth, being in time is always involved in varying degrees in the knowledge which it possesses. The subject is never totally dissociated from the object which it cognizes. This kind of truth can never be emphasized enough in a world in which the worship of science constantly encourages the notion that there exists a pure, scientific objectivity which could be applied to all aspects of human life, even to the establishment of a code of ethics, as if moral behaviour could be measured by scientific criteria, and as if scientists were Olympians, impartial creatures who were as objective in their judgments as the ideal instruments which are the accepted references for our system of weights and measures. This is of course an illusion, to say nothing of the fact that scientists are no more moral, honest or kind than the average forked animal. They are just as cannibalistic, petty and jaundiced as the bulk of mankind.

Evil and suffering are endured at the individuated level of being, and they are part of the process of birth, growth, decay and death of men, and of the instinctual killing of the animal world. Creation, that is to say being in time, in its various individuations (with the exception of its essence which rejoins

Being and perfection) is finite and therefore imperfect. Indeed its journey, or progress, through time is the means by which it sheds its dross, its finitude and imperfections, until it is left with the embers or Essence, fit for eternity and pure Being. Being knows essence as essence, but it only knows it fully and perfectly once the individuated essence has returned to Being—once it has, through existence, realized the essence of its individuation through becoming and time, and has become the true essence which it was destined to be and will for ever be, that is to say (excluding any untenable notions of original sin, limbo, purgatory or hell) once it has reached the required degree of purity and perfection which will give it its final and adequate place within Being. That does not mean that Being contains impure essences, and is therefore imperfect, it means that just as there are varying degrees of intensity of heat and light in the sun, so it is with Being, and that Being which knows itself as essence completes its knowledge of itself and its perfection through individuated essence in time, which is part of Eternity.

Being is therefore not static, closed and unevolving, but becoming. It does not change, it knows itself. Individuated essence is a necessary part of Being. It does not become perfect, since it is already perfect; it realizes its own continuous perfection through becoming. Hegel quotes Heraclitus as saying: 'All is becoming,' and Hegel continues: 'This becoming is *the* principle. This is implied in the expression: "Being is not more than not-being." The becoming is and also is not. Purely opposed determinations are tied up in one unity, which contains being as well as not-being. It is a great discovery to have recognized that being and not-being are only abstractions without truth, and that the basic truth is the becoming. The understanding isolates the two as true and valid; on the other hand, Reason recognizes both, it recognizes that one contains the other and that it is the whole, the absolute which must be determined as becoming . . . Heraclitus was the first to formulate the notion of the infinite. The first to conceive of nature as infinite in itself and its essence as process. With him began the existence of philosophy."[18]

The individuation which through actualization returns to the whole and to Being does not become fully submerged or unrecognizably lost in it. It retains its essential traits, affinities and relationships with other essences. In other words, Being and Eternity do not turn individuations into a totally nondescript whole, in which everything is absolutely, unchangingly the same. The sameness lies in the fact that the component elements are all essences, part of the becoming of Being, but each essence achieves, through becoming, its necessary relationship with other essences, and the relationship immanently established finds its place and is maintained in transcendence and Being which is the means or mediator through which individuated essences fully recognize themselves, know themselves, and are eternally realized in their relationship. In this way, God or Being does not abolish individuations, but reveals and maintains what is eternally true in being. That is to say the nature or essence of being is to realize the possibilities of the entities which have the necessary aptitudes for realization, and these realizations shed their subjective or individual elements, and become objective and immortal, when they return to Being which, since in itself it neither becomes nor perishes, cannot be objectified in entities which take part in becoming. This point ought to make it impossible to look upon the relationship between God or Being and becoming as pantheism, for the essence of this relationship is that Being cannot be objectified in becoming; it certainly objectifies or eternalizes and knows itself through its actualizations, but it is not absolutely coeval with becoming, any more than the Logos is absolutely coeval with God.

I mentioned earlier the equation in Greek thought of *ratio*, reason, logos, with necessity. Reason, or necessity, is the organizing element of life, what Bergson—for whom reason is both the absolute substance of creation and the truth that knows itself—called, for those who read him with an open mind, the 'élan vital', the force of creative energy and urge towards a fuller life which is both the end of reason and the necessity of life. It is also Platonic reason, the urge towards the understanding of things, the motive force or essence of Being being to know itself through creation. The importance of reason—logos—necessity, was discovered by the Greeks, and their importance in thought in general cannot be exaggerated. I always return to the view expressed by Whitehead, that Western thought is only a series of footnotes to Plato, who sums up both the pre-Socratic philosophers and Socrates himself, and also expresses in his philosophy thoughts which are part of Middle Eastern and Eastern philosophy. 'Faith in reason,' Whitehead said, 'is the trust that the ultimate natures of things lie together, in a harmony which excludes mere arbitrariness. It is the faith that at the basis of things we shall not find mere arbitrary mystery.'[19] Reason or necessity precludes arbitrariness, and 'the doctrine of necessity in universality means that there is an essence which forbids relationships by and as violations of its rationality; speculative philosophy seeks that essence.'[20]

Although I said at the beginning that this work will not carry any critique of great philosophers of the past, not-infrequent quotations from, or references to, Plato, Kant, Hegel, Whitehead and Einstein will make it evident that these philosophers and thinkers have illumined my way, have seen much farther than I ever could, and have described what they have seen with greater precision and depth than I could ever hope to achieve. This, as previously suggested, does not preclude attempts to say something about the problems with which I am concerned, any more than the fact that the Himalayas have been climbed will preclude other attempts to do so. It is in the nature of the human mind to try over and over again to overcome certain obstacles. None is more difficult, nor more tempting, than the problem of the origins of life and of religion. Man tries to give birth to great ideas, and man tries to destroy them, but great ideas never die, any more than great religions. What we discard matters practically as much as what we adopt, though there is no way backwards. Neither philosophy nor religion ever returns to past stages, once a great step forward has been taken. The historical past is not reversible; on the plane of the glory of great builders or destroyers of religions, and important philosophers, there is no retracing of steps. Once Jove had dethroned Chronos and the Titans, none of them could ever return to Olympus. What has been said by Plato or Hegel can neither be gainsaid nor effaced; it can only be transcended, or partly replaced by another great philosophy or philosophies, which would have to sum up Plato or Hegel and subsume them in order to have any social or historical value. (This is the case, for example, with Marxism, which has transcended certain aspects of Hegelianism, but which has not yet been transcended and therefore is still vital in our times.) It is the same with religion; there are no mutations in history and time, there is only rational, ineluctable necessity.

Men may not see this, because they find it most difficult to see what stares them in the face, or they may, notwithstanding their assertion of objectivity, be as subjective as is normal, and try to discard or ignore what they dislike or fear. The fact is that the universe is fundamentally, irretrievably rational, and that if the human mind is given its chance it will, as part of the universe and endowed with the same structure, discover progressively and steadily the truth of the world in which it lives. It will discover the truth of the world as part of its becoming in which it participates, up to the point which its finitude enables it to reach, but not beyond. The world shows everywhere repetitions and similarities of certain structures. This pattern includes the animal world and the human organism, and it stands to reason that the human mind, human reason, an essential part of the necessity which animates the universe, contains or is made up of structures and forms which must be analogous to those of nature and of things, and which, therefore, must make it possible to have a growing re-cognition between the essence of reason and the essence of things. This re-cognition is the task of the philosopher, the scientist and the artist.

This similarity of structure between the world and mind must not be turned into the Berkeleyan notion that only the world of the mind exists, and that the world is purely and simply the subject's representation. One must, I think, adopt the very reasonable Kantian notion that the objective world is constructed by the subject experiencing it according to its innate structures and categories. The mind is a synthesizing activity; the categories are criteria of interpretation for realistic experience. Kant shares the Platonic principle that if any rational understanding is to be possible, the reason in man must be akin to the reason in things. Locke and Descartes held similar views, with the difference that God was for them the mediator between the reason in man and the reason in things. We are back to St Augustine's logos as mediator between man and the understanding of the universe. Faith in reason and the rationality of the universe is not confined to pre-twentieth-century thought. Einstein, the great thinker of modern times, said: 'I believe in a world ruled by laws which I try to apprehend in a widely speculative manner.' Einstein never accepted the view that reality could be reduced to probabilities and statistics; and in that context it is interesting to see that Heisenberg himself, referring to Planck's quantum theory, says: 'In recent years many investigations have been concerned with these difficulties [i.e. concerning the attempt to arrive at a mathematical formulation of the interaction of the elementary particles], but so far no one has been able to arrive at a satisfactory solution. The only consolation is the assumption that in very small regions of space-time of the order of magnitude of the elementary particles, the notions of space and time become unclear, i.e. in very small intervals even the concepts "earlier" and "later" can no longer be properly defined. Of course nothing is altered in space-time on the large scale, but we must bear in mind the possibility that experiment may well prove that small-scale space-time processes may run in reverse to the causal sequence.

It is here that the latest developments of atomic physics once again come up against the question of causal laws. It is too early to say whether this will lead to new paradoxes, or that new deviations from causal laws will appear. Perhaps our attempts to formulate the laws of elementary particles mathematically will lead to new possibilities enabling us to avoid these difficulties. However, even now it has become quite certain that the latest developments in atomic physics will once more have repercussions in the sphere of philosophy. The final answer to the questions we have just posed will only come with the mathematical formulation of the natural laws governing the behaviour of elementary particles; when, for instance, we shall know why it is that the proton happens to be precisely 1836 times as heavy as the electron.'[21] The impossibility of ascertaining at the same time the velocity and the position of a given particle is neither final nor a proof of random behaviour, there is still a certain element which renders possible the establishment of precise statistical laws; secondly, this statistical aspect of particles' behaviour does not affect the large-scale processes of behaviour in the life of the universe. All this boils down to the fact that the statistical behaviour of extremely small particles with practically no mass and no time-life is without effect in the life of large space-time regions in which order prevails.

Einstein believed that form and structure were repeated in the universe and that man could apprehend them. The idea or form is the abstract structure or image as a projection of reality in the mind, which is thus enabled to re-cognize reality. Essential thought or ideas are undying; they survive the pressure of their opposites, or they unite with them in new syntheses, leaving behind them remainders for new developments. Thought as idea is in fact an abstract or symbolic representation of forms, which are the essential structures of reality, facts, events or experiences, and which mind apprehends according to its affinities with them. That is to say, if there is no structural correspondence between mind and the real, there cannot be any apprehension of it. Natural science tells us nothing of the essential structure of things; it is purely concerned with the way things work and the way they are related phenomenologically. Abstractions or ideas, of course, do not exist separately in their own right. They only exist as part of the whole which is the mind, or the whole which is Being. In the case of Being, becoming can only mean the eternal and continuous breaking up of the one into the many, and the final coming together of these fragments or parts into the one. That was the view of Empedocles, as well as of Hegel and Whitehead, though not quite that of Plato, for whom becoming was not the true reality, but only the *maya* or appearance of true reality, unchanging and eternal.

Still, whether the becoming is only appearance, or is the actualization of the eternal, the fundamental point common to both attitudes is that the real essence of a thing is synonymous with the constitution of its structure. On this score even Locke, who could not by any stretch of the imagination be described as a Platonist or an idealist, agreed. All things have a structure which coordinates their finality, and whether one describes this finality as teleological or 'teleonomic' is irrelevant. As Whitehead quotes Francis Bacon: 'All bodies whatsoever, though they have no sense, yet they have perception, for when one body is applied to another there is a kind of election to embrace that which is agreeable, and to exclude or expel that which is ingrate.'[22] When an existential entity, be it an organism or a work of art, has achieved totality or wholeness, it means that each element and nothing more can contribute adequately to the harmony of the whole. Locke said: 'This is certain, things, however absolute and entire they seem in themselves, are but retainers to other parts of nature for that which they are most taken notice of by us. Their observable qualities, actions and powers are owing to something without them; and there is not so complete and perfect a part that we know of nature, which does not owe the being it has, and the excellencies of it, to its neighbours.'[23] He further says: 'When we find out

an idea, by whose intervention we discover the connexion of
two others, this is a revelation from God to us, by the voice of
reason; for we then come to know a truth that we did not know
before. When God declares any truth to us, this is a revelation
to us by the voice of his spirit, and we are advanced in our
knowledge.'[24]

Change, process, becoming is therefore of the essence of
Being, yet how then can the passing of things exhibit permanence? It can do so only according to the forms or essences
which inform them. The forms are transcendent and timeless,
and their essence is to realize their potential through existence
and actualization. Actualization implies elimination of all possibilities and virtualities which could, in various degrees, lay
claims to actualization. There is no more addition to the eternal
than there is addition to the total matter of the universe. Being,
for Plato, is anything with the capacity of acting or of being
acted upon. 'O Heavens,' says he, 'can we ever be made to believe that motion and life, soul and mind are not present with
absolute Being? Can we imagine Being to be devoid of life and
to remain in awful unmeaningness, an everlasting fixture?'
Being contains the necessary motives for life and mind to realize
themselves in time, and if it were not so there could be no
possible explanation for existence.

Any individuated entity has both a relationship with other
entities and an essence which relates to the primordial essence.
Nothing exists by itself, or can exist by itself. Life in all its
aspects implies solidarity with and the need for others, irrespective of the instinct for survival which, at the natural level, can
also crush or destroy others. Yet these manifestations only take
place as part of the intricacy and inter-relatedness of creation.
Some things fall, some things rise, some have only a moment,
a day or a year or so to live, and are consumed by others which
in their turn are also consumed. Some mesons live only for a
fraction of a second, yet they have their place in the universe, in
which, as Shakespeare said, 'there is a special Providence in the
fall of a sparrow.' The organicity, the wholeness of life cannot

be conceived of in any other terms. 'To be', said St Augustine, 'is no other than to be one, in so far, therefore, that anything attains unity, in so far, it is.' The fundamental attributes of organicity and wholeness are coherence and absolute congruence with the essence of the whole organism. Without these there is only fragmentation and appearance without life. Essential entities change in appearance, but not in substance, and they retain their relationship with other entities and their place in the universe. 'Essence or form is', says Aristotle, 'a certain type of structure organized for a certain end.' This end is actualization. Any actualization contains the sufficient reasons for which this actualization is so, and these reasons can only be apprehended by imagination, and not by the understanding. Each individuation is internally determined, and yet has a phenomenal appearance of freedom. Therefore a thing, in the end, can only be what it is. (This statement is neither verifiable nor refutable at the empirical level, though it is meaningful.) Both history and thought unfold along a pattern which can only be known once it has been completed. Blind chance, hazard, random creativity, will produce nothing. There must be and there is a sufficient reason or cause for everything, and this cause carries its own finality or subjective aims which determine the affinities, assimilations and coherence of the whole thing. There is, of course, at the start a wide field of possibilities out of which actualizations take place. Whatever is not actualized has nevertheless its value as a non-actualized element, which can always come into actualization if the forces or causes which rejected it disappear or are weakened enough for this to be possible. In that case, the new actualization will change its shape and therefore maintain in being forces contained in it which keep other non-actualized elements at bay. And this will go on and on, in a continuous process of change and interactions between being and non-being. Once a thing is, it remains an entity which plays a part in all realized entities. An essential thought or idea, that is to say a projection of true reality, lives on, through transformations, until the end of history and time. Everything that is, is a manifestation or an actualization of an aspect of the original or primordial essence of Being, which can only be known through these various actualizations and their relationship with it.

3

Society, Religion and Being

Creation does not of course proceed along one single line or narrow stream, but always, as it were, on a broad front or flood, seeking many openings, many passages, involving various orders or aspects of life which grow, develop and decay, to be replaced by others. Any order which succeeds another necessarily carries with it the elements which have absorbed and replaced the former one, and marks therefore a progression towards a better capability for survival and greater complexity, and therefore a widening of the knowledge of the possibilities of creation. Although orders, societies, civilizations are not copies one from the other, they have characteristics shared by all which constitute the essential elements or laws of development of nature and of creation. There are therefore basic determining laws, and there are phenomenal aspects of these laws which change and decay according to contingencies, circumstances, organic transformations or the social and political problems of the society or epoch they are part of. The individuated entities of these societies or epochs select or retain what they need according to their inherent affinities and subjective aims, within a climate which may be favourable or unfavourable to them. Those to which the climate is favourable grow with it and manifest their appearance in it. Those to which it is not, retain their individuality and, proceeding as it were underground, dialectically absorb what is unfavourable or apparently opposed to them, and prepare the rejection of the order which does not enable them to manifest themselves openly, and its replacement by an order which will evolve from the elements which are alien to it and which work actively for its rejection and for the establishment of the coincidence of appearance with substance or form.

A society, though very disparate in composition, forms a whole, but not of course a whole like a human body which is an organic entity or integrated organism with a self-caused finality. A society is a composite whole, a space-time continuum of many magnetic fields harmonized by the epoch to which they belong, and this harmony includes melodies, fugues and counterpoints which at times may sound like cacophonous parts of the whole. There are moments when a society acts as a whole, that is to say moments when what could be called its true mind, its spirit or *Zeitgeist* emerges and calls for a single, concerted type of action in order to survive, that is to say in order to maintain the dominant ethos or essence of this society, established by history and embodying the essential inheritance, traditions and aspirations which constitute the *raison d'être* and finality of the society.

These moments are rare, and the essential elements of a given society can only become part of the consciousness of this society in moments of crisis, when everyday preoccupations and phenomenality are suddenly reduced to the essence which in this case coincides with the preservation of the society which they have established. At this point it may come in conflict with the essence of other societies animated, as it is itself, with the essence to survive and to assert their dominance over this apparent conflict of orders. The process by which one society eliminates or replaces another is the same process by which an entity accepts or rejects the possible elements from which it actualizes itself. The elements which, in the end, would militate against organized developments of life and creation are discarded and, through trial and error, reabsorbed into new societies which must necessarily progress towards the ultimate essence of Being which is total self-knowledge.

This does not imply a purely pragmatic morality based upon

success. It means, on the contrary, that every individuated entity, as well as every society, must seek out, with the utmost care, what its true essence is, and if it does so, it will necessarily discover that its true essence conforms with the true essence of Being, that it is growth and not destruction that matters, unless destruction tends towards growth, and that all elements which militate against it are slowly and finally eliminated, whether through their own violence or through organic processes, both being part of the dialectics of nature and creation. One must hasten to say that the violence of nature is not tinged with evil, that is to say it is spontaneous, natural or instinctive, without any consciousness of itself, and exists purely as part of a natural process of rise and fall, birth, death and rebirth, in order finally to reach pure Being. Creation rises from Being, full of possibilities, actualizes itself through time which enables actualizations to reach pure Being, and relegates the discarded possibilities to the realm of non-being.

The passage from the infinite virtualities of pure Being or the matrix of things to determinations and individuations, takes place through forms. Out of Being's infinite flow of virtualities, individuations take on appearances at diverse times and places, yet all are informed with the substance which gave them life. The domain of virtualities is the domain of being and not non-being. It is the continuum of Descartes from which life takes place, and it is life which creates non-being. Time is part of Being, coeval with it, and is the becoming or process of growth through which creation returns to Being. 'Time,' as Plato said, 'is the moving image of Eternity.' Time is therefore the element in which eternal forms or essences take determined shapes and characters, and through the process of becoming, achieve the finality which is the search for the perfect form. This finality is determined by the kind of structure which everything, from the atom to non-organic entities, contains. The greater and greater complexity of the entities involved rests upon the greater and greater harmonization of the basic structures which are precise and, with the exception of infinitesimally small par-

D

ticles (the behaviour of which is only statistical), subject to unchanging mathematical laws.

Creation is an ever more complex interplay of organisms,
each with a strictly structurally-determined pattern, which not
only repeat one another at various levels, but also interlock
at various levels, in intricate, yet perfectly unmistakable, order.
This order is the order of reason (for unless it were reasonable,
it would not be order) which may yet contain elements of disorder or improbabilities. If it did not, Being would be entirely
composed of positive aspects of things, and that would mean
staticity and lack of movement, that is to say non-Being. Being
contains all aspects of things, the positive and the negative
figuring all possibilities of appearances capable of actualization.
The essences contain all possibilities, to be moulded by time
into images of Eternity. Therefore order is also the master or
overall co-ordinator of disorder which is as necessary as night
is necessary to day, bad to good, and finite to infinite. Any one
of these opposites by itself would simply be a closed, uniform
totality, that is to say nothingness or non-Being. 'The genera-
tion of our world came about from a combination of necessity
with understanding, but understanding overrules necessity by
persuading her to conduct the most part of the effects to the
best issue . . . whence if a man would tell the tale of the making
truly, he must bring the errant cause also into the story.'
(Plato.)[1]

The rationality of the world supplies its final consolation, in
virtue of which creativity passed from virtuality to being in
Time in a world of relativeness. The rational, or the good, is the
sustaining cause of all things. 'Good' is used here in the sense
of congruency to the original or essential structure of being.
Each perfection reached through existence adds to the final
harmony of Eternity.

Not only Plato and Aristotle, but practically every great
philosopher from Hobbes to Locke, Kant and Hegel, thought
that the rational was also the good. Kant sums them all up with
the words: 'Reason will yet go to Nature not as a scholar who

only recites what his teacher wishes, but as a judge having authority who compels witnesses to answer the questions he puts to them.'[2] The world order is both rational and good, in the absolute—it is men that are neither totally good nor totally rational, they are a mixture of both good and bad, rational and irrational, and therefore these ethical attributes are, on the human plane, relative values. 'But whatsoever is the object of any man's Appetite or Desire; that is it, which he for his part calleth *Good*: And the object of his Hate, and Aversion, *Evil*; and of his Contempt, *Vile* and *Inconsiderable*. For these words of Good, Evil, and Contemptible, are ever used with relation to the person that useth them: There being nothing simply and absolutely so; nor any common Rule of Good and Evil, to be taken from the nature of the objects themselves . . .'[3]

Eternity, Being, God, the Creator, like any other creator, makes himself through his work and only knows himself through his work. In all these cases the important elements are harmony, order, congruence with the whole, faithfulness to the inner structure and the finality of the work; and of course what is aesthetically satisfying, what conforms to these above-mentioned canons, is also morally good, for the achievement of perfect harmony, the satisfying of the divine laws of music or the mathematics of Pythagoras and Plato, is also the realization of the primal aim of the creator. The unknowing to which we come in the end is, according to Eckhart, an unknowing beyond, not beneath knowing, so that rational explanation must go on being pushed to its furthest limits.

Religion cannot be dismissed as being merely an emotional feeling, an irrational urge to compensate for fears and mysteries which we cannot comprehend, and which compels us to forge deities and rites in order to conjure away our terrors and to protect and comfort ourselves. This is a simplistic view, however powerful the mind which expounds it, be it that of Freud or that of the average scientist or of scientifically obsessed men who think that because they know that DNA gives the required instructions to the cells, they themselves can give instructions to the DNA. Religion is a human need as vital as the sap to the tree, and those iconoclasts who demolish the churches and statues of the old faith do so in the name of science or adopt new ones which are, on the whole, far more dehumanized and destructive than the ones which they have repudiated. Materialism, deterministic or non-deterministic, Marxist or chance-ridden, scientism, fixation on objectivity and so-called scientific truths, these are the nourishing milk of all fanatics from Robespierre to St Just and other apostles of radical reforms, far more dangerous to man than the simple yet according to them fetish-ridden, love of Mother Teresa of India who does not speak about but practises truth and loves a humankind no doubt obtuse and superstitious in some cases, but more in need of affection and understanding than of scientific demystification. Religion is no doubt a feeling, a belief, and not a mathematically verifiable truth, but it is not irrational, it is part of reason, as seen by thinkers from Plato to Kant, Hegel, Kierkegaard, Jaspers, Maritain and Einstein, and it is the most basic human experience, that which has lifted man from all fours to the forked, standing-up position. It has helped him to walk, gazing upward, out of his dark, primordial caves to the cities where he now finds shelter and protection against the illnesses which once decimated mankind, and hopes for a better life.

Whatever form it may take, religion determines our lives and shapes our characters and actions. 'Its concepts', as Whitehead put it, 'though derived primarily from special experience, are yet of universal validity, to be offered by faith to our ordering of all experiences.'[4] In another place Whitehead seems to me to put admirably the rationality and consequently the necessity of religion: 'Religion is an ultimate craving to infuse into the insistent particularity of emotion that non-temporal generality which primarily belongs to conceptual thought alone. In the higher organisms the differences of tempo between the mere emotions and the conceptual experiences produce a life-tedium, unless this supreme fusion has been effected. The two sides of the organism require a reconciliation in which emotional experiences illustrate a conceptual justification, conceptual experiences find an emotional justification.'⁵ This fusion can only be attempted by a religion which is rationally acceptable, or rather which is acceptable to reason. From Aquinas to Locke, Pascal, Bergson and Teilhard de Chardin, religious thinkers have tried to meet this requirement. The failure to effect such a reconciliation can only produce a divided sensibility, oscillating between total solipsism and destructive and lame rationalism on the one hand, and mystical emotionalism on the other, as was the case in the latter half of the nineteenth century. So thought and emotions were separated, thought coming to mean simply ratiocination, while emotions, unprocessed by mind, turned into sentiments and sentimentality. Such a division of the human person precludes great art or a unified society capable of confronting its problems as a whole. Reason deprived of its metaphysical roots, its sense of the sacredness of the human personality, turns to self-worship.

4

Why Being?

How can one answer the question: why is there Being and
what is Being? One cannot define Being *a priori*, because it
obviously is not an entity, an object, a fact, determined, limited
and bound. Whatever it is, it is not that, for if it were, it would
be finite. Being is therefore neither definable, nor endowed with
any attributes or characteristics which necessarily imply limitations. One can define its manifestations, its appearances, its
phenomenal individuations, but not Being itself. Yet, since
those things are, there must be a reason for their being; if not,
they would not be, and the reason, the cause of their being,
must necessarily be in Being, or be part of Being. Therefore
there is one and only one aspect of characterization of Being
which one can put forward, and that is that Being is necessary creativity. Having said this, one may ask why Being
should be necessary. The reply is, I am afraid, merely tauto-
logical: that unless it were necessary, it would not be. Why it
is so cannot be explained, except by saying that without this
character of necessity, there would be no creativity, and no
creation.

This character of necessity applied to Being and, therefore,
to creation, does not by any stretch of the imagination mean
absolutely predictable and individually guided determinism. Far
from it. Creativity does not take place from one definite point,
along an already traced line and towards a fixed end. Creativity
takes place on a vast scale, without a definite, clear-cut beginning; it takes place on a broad front, and with a simultaneity of

events which is neither linear nor circumscribed by a given place nor purely limited to the events which emerge into consciousness or into existence. Thence the hits and misses of creativity, its false starts, its dead ends, yet all within the context of necessity and as part of necessity. Whatever is endowed with insufficient positive essence, or whatever is merely virtuality, as a negative part of being, without sufficient essence and without a finality of its own, can nevertheless achieve a brief emergence in life, as a part of negativity and necessary non-being, but does not achieve true being, and consequently fails to become part of Being. If Being were absolutely perfect, omniscient, omni-present, complete in essence and existence, there could not be any creation. Being or God diminishes Himself through creation in order to complete Himself. God-made man restores to God the essence he has taken from Him, once it has been made, through God's gift of grace, fit for Eternity. In Simone Weil's words (*First and Last Notebooks*, 1970): 'Every man, seeing himself from the point of view of God the creator, should regard his own existence as a sacrifice made by God. I am God's abdication. The more I exist, the more God abdicates. So if I take God's side rather than my own I ought to regard my existence as a diminution, a decrease.'[1]

The dogma which makes of God or Being a separate entity from creation is a logical impossibility. If God is complete, perfect, instead of completing and perfecting and knowing Himself, through creation, there is no possible explanation for creation and time. For the notion that either time or creation began at a certain time or moment, within Eternity, necessarily prompts the question: why did it take place at that chosen time and not at another? And, if God as entity is separated from creation as entity, then where is the cause, where is the urge to create, why at a certain time and not at another, where were the materials for creation taken from, and where were they if they were separated from Being or from God, and if they were not, at what moment, if moment there was, did they begin to be activated for creation? Such notions obviously posit impossible dialectics between Time and Eternity, between Being and being, Creator and created, and they merely prompt the conclusion that these entities cannot be separated the one from the other. Creation is inherent and necessary to Being, as Christ was, and is, necessary to God. These entities are inseparable, and in both cases the journey through time is the necessary part of the perfection of Being, which has to go through Time and existence in order to know itself or Himself absolutely both in positive and negative aspects.

Christ is not therefore a means for God to redeem mankind, whose only original sin, if sin there is, is to have been created, but a means for God to know Himself through knowing what His creation knows through life, suffering and death, and, through being, to be partly known to His human creation which could only know Him or apprehend Him in this incarnation in human form. God could neither know Himself, nor be known by, nor know, His creation, except through incarnation. He only knew the essence of being, and only knew Himself as essence, a knowledge which has to be completed through the actualization or existentialization of essence. In a similar way, man can only know God through the incarnation, or in rare moments of ineffable, mystical union with Him. Creation, like Christ, is part of the Eternal, which unfolds according to its inner laws, and not part of an act of choice or decision at a so-called moment of time, and for a given purpose.

Being is becoming, and God or transcendence is immanent in creation and will be so until the process is completed by the total actualization of all the positive aspects of the possibilities and virtualities of creativity, intent upon actualization and existence through time, in order to go beyond time, to pure Being and Eternity. In the words of A. N. Whitehead: 'It is not the case that there is an actual world which accidentally happens to exhibit an order of nature. If there were no order, there would be no world.'[2] Being and creation are one, just as God and creation are one, united by the same causation and the same finality. Creation is continuous change and separation of being from non-being. What is transient, purely subjective, that is to say lacking in essence, becomes non-being; what is, that is to say the true actualization of essence, is objectified and becomes part of Being or part of God's eternal knowledge of Himself. Knowledge of essence is in fact pure self-knowledge, therefore ideal knowledge. Knowledge requires the realization of essence, the actualization of forms which reach the perfection which God knows, and by knowing it He knows Himself. What becomes eternal is what achieves perfection through Time. Thence the importance of Time, the present and existence.

The laws which preside over the working of creation and the universe are unchanging, immutable, objective, if one uses this word in the sense of *in-se* (in-itself), that is to say they are what they are, unmodified, unprocessed by the *per-se* (or for-itself) of being. Every being has or possesses an essential structure which has affinities with certain other essential structures of creation and of nature, and therefore is equipped to apprehend any one of them and to reveal it in its existential appearance which embodies the essential structure of both. It is not therefore a question of making, or strictly speaking of creating, something out of nothing or out of chaos, but of *re-cognizing* essential truths. The laws of nature are undeniably, by definition, objective, but the way the human being approaches them in order to discover them, or uses them once discovered, never is. 'Science always presupposes the existence of man,' as Niels Bohr has said, and 'we must become conscious of the fact that we are not merely observers, but also actors on the stage of life.'[3] Each human being approaches and uses the laws of nature according to his own inner structure. These laws, verifiable by experiment, therefore objective in themselves, cannot be used as analogies to measure accurately the workings of the human mind and of human affectivity, in its social or individual manifestations, in the aesthetic or in the ethical field. That could only be so if one accepted the widespread scientific, or one should rather say, pseudo-scientific, notion that there is nothing except being. I use the word pseudo-scientific to make

the point that if this notion were truly demonstrable and verifiable by experiment, then it would be truly scientific in the
exact meaning of the term. As it is not possible that there
should be nothing else, except being, without cause or finality,
this is a merely pseudo-scientific notion which pertains to
the domain of belief and dogmatics which some scientists
hotly repudiate, and the existence of which they prefer to
ignore.

One cannot think of being without Being, that is to say without movement from, and towards, Being. If being were thought
of in isolation, it would be a static, self-contained, closed, mona-
dic manifestation which would have to be self-caused and with
its own end. It could be mechanistically cyclical, or pure and
simply endless, and even these two absurd notions cannot manage to exclude the notion of going beyond, and of transcendence, which is Being. If there were only being without Being,
being would have to be self-caused and continuous, or be merely
a brief and spontaneous emergence from non-Being to which
it would be condemned to return in a state of eternal nothingness. So that, in fact, the source of the essence of being, or
one could say the cause of being, would be nothingness, and its
finality would also be nothingness—a manifest absurdity, for
nothingness is not-Being, and something which is the cause and
finality of being cannot be nothingness.

Whatever one might say, and irrespective of any noble and
stoic poses one might strike, the life of being in such conditions
could only be totally nihilistic and dominated by a purely relativistic morality. This would be to ignore the longing for, and
the sense of, the infinite which we know to have been part of
man since the history of man was known. Man has always felt
that there is something more, something beyond himself, not his
fears, his anxieties, but a mystery and a finality of which he is
part and to which it is his categorical moral duty to contribute.
This feeling of transcendence is, all in all, as much part of the
structure of his mind and spirit as the life which he possesses
and which he wishes to continue to possess for as long as

possible, unless he is too ill mentally or physically to wish for anything except the sleep of the womb.

Life without such hopes, such beliefs, can only be a twilight life, the life of Marcus Aurelius, in a crumbling empire and city, a mysterious distant smile, among ruins, in a world without meaning or a sense of human brotherhood. In such cases, the singular and noble individual, whether he is Marcus Aurelius or Nietzsche, can manage to live on the verge of the void, and find in it enough exhilaration to sustain him in his tragic plight, enough to live a noble life, though even his detachment from it, and the little importance he attaches to it, are, alas, taken up as examples by baser minds and empty hearts, in order to establish domination over their fellow beings or to treat them with disdain. Besides that, there is the fact that the continuous confrontation of being with nothingness, that is to say, the denial of past and future, compels life to be lived at the level of an intense and isolated subjectivism, that is to say without any possibility of intersubjectivity.

But effects cannot be used to explain causes, that is to say, one cannot use the argument that being deprived of Being would make life entirely nihilistic and that this cannot possibly be so, for if it were so, life would be absurd, stupid, cruel, etc. That would be an argument which, up to a point, would obviously be derived by analogy from the ontological argument. One must start from the facts, and ask oneself why there is being, and how being could come about. The proof of the existence of the world, starting from the premise that Being or God could not be perfect unless it existed, obviously has no value for scientific thought. This kind of scholastic sophistry can indeed be rejected, though neither Leibnitz nor Kant did so without very serious cogitations. But the argument that since the world exists, there must necessarily be some cause for its existence, is not the ontological argument over again, and yet some scientists reject it on the same ground of unscientific lack of verifiability, using all sorts of simplistic, pejorative terms to explain their decisions. True, no scientific proof of the cause of the existence of Being can be given, except that there is being.

Yet the scientists who reject Being are no more disinterested, no more detached or supposedly objective than those who believe in it. They are on the contrary just as biased, belief-ridden, subjective, as anyone else; the difference is that while everyone else knows that one cannot help being subjective, they evidently believe that they are truly objective. So we are back to the story of the Cretan liar. Do we lie when we know that we lie? Are we objective when we think that we are objective? Certainly not, since this thought is subjective, and since scientists are no more free from subjectivity than other men. Besides, the scientist's worship of facts, his belief that to know is to be able to do, and that knowledge is necessarily good, or the basis of good and morality, coupled with a certain lack of imagination (except, of course, in the case of the truly great scientists like Einstein and a few others), makes of the average scientist as poor a judge of morality and political or religious beliefs as the average human being, who has on the other hand the advantage of being less certain about the truth—moral or religious—and is therefore more likely to develop the necessary receptivity to encounter it.

In order that there might be being, there must necessarily be order at the macroscopic as well as the microscopic level, irrespective of some unpredictability in the behaviour of practically massless particles. From the dawn of philosophy to modern times the greatest thinkers have all thought so. Anaximander was, if not the first, one of the first to say so: 'The cause of the birth of all things is also the cause of their end, as it is just that it should be so, for they must make an end and expiate for their mutual injustice in the order of time.' The whole of Greek thought, which played a vital part in Christianity, a part at least as important as that of Judaism, rests upon the supremacy of reason. Greek mysticism and idealism not only dominated the early centuries of Christianity, but they also retained their importance in the Augustinian synthesis of Greek thought and Judaic existentialism. And it is above all Greek rationalism, with reason seen as both the organizational element of life and the basis of the search for the true understanding of things, which forms the cornerstone of Western technological developments and, to a large extent, of Western civilization. Neither the Judaic complex of guilt nor the Roman legalism and power structure could displace the pride and the dreams of reason which we have inherited from the Greeks. As everything has its obverse, it is also rationalism, or, to be precise, lame rationalism, one-eyed reason, as A. N. Whitehead put it, which is responsible for the attempted dethronement of reason in the Western world. Aquinas with his conviction that reason leads to faith, Kant with his faith in the supremacy of reason, Hegel with his bold Platonic assertion that the rational is the real, Leibnitz with his view that the world is rational, all insist upon the fact that the world is subject to order. Descartes says so repeatedly: 'The strength of the argument which I have used rests upon the fact that I know that it would not be possible for my nature to be what it is, that is to say, that I should have in myself the idea of God, if God did not exist.'[4] Leibnitz says something similar when he claims that the idea of God is inherent in man. We could not, in fact, think of the absolute if we did not have some notion of the absolute in ourselves. Even Sartre has to concede that 'man's basic desire is to be God'.[5] Yet is the idea, or the dream of a thing, or even its possible existence, enough to make this thing real? Kant dealt with this argument; it does not need to be repeated. The answer depends on what the thing or the notion dreamt of is. At first, it might look as if one posited the existence of a given thing because there was a universal desire for it. This of course is not enough; beliefs change throughout history, and the belief in the need for the absolute, however widespread it may be, could change.

The universal longing for an idea is not a proof of the reality or existence of this idea. Yet if being were purely contingent and had no relation with transcendence, being would not be able

to have any idea of transcendence. 'If I were absolutely independent, if I were the cause of my being . . . I should not lack
any perfection whatsoever, for I should have given myself all
those I have some idea about in myself, and then I should be
God.' (Descartes.)[6] Existent being is not therefore self-caused;
it is contingent and dependent upon immanence and transcendence. 'If God has imprinted the notion of Himself on every man,'
asks Descartes, 'how is it that men have such different notions
of Him?'[7]

The fact is that God is part of creation and history, therefore,
though His essence is part of man, He reveals himself progressively and differently to man, according to time and place, and
above all according to the means which men have of apprehending Him. This is not, as some would have it, a merely anthropomorphic conception of God, it is that of a continuous relationship between Being or God and man, a relationship which by
nature is changing, growing and developing. Bergson said: 'The
nature of God will thus appear in the very reasons that one has
for believing in His existence.'[8] Inspiration or grace cannot blow
at random; it requires a certain state of receptivity. It certainly
cannot blow on Sartre, who declares that 'being is without
reasons, without causes, without necessity'.[9] One wonders how
a representative of such an irrational, chance-created breed can
reach such would-be rational pronouncements, and by what
magic he expects to have them accepted, since we are by his
definition an absurd and useless passion on earth. Jean Rostand,
a greater genius than Sartre, avoids Sartre's aggressive atheism
and, on the contrary, gives his own a touch of noble and controlled stoicism: 'Derisory atom, lost in the lifeless, infinite
universe, man knows that his feverish activity is only a local-
ized, ephemeral, insignificant, aimless phenomenon. He knows
that his values are only valid for himself, and that from the
point of view of the stars, the fall of an empire, the destruction
of an ideal, matter no more than the destruction of an ant-heap
caused by the footsteps of an absent-minded passer-by. Therefore . . . avoiding the sterile vertigo of the infinite, deaf to the

fearful silence of space, he will endeavour to become as un-
cosmic as the cosmos is inhuman; fiercely turned in upon himself, he will devote himself humbly, earthily, humanly, to the
accomplishment of his puny designs, to which he will devote
the same seriousness as if they were intent on eternal ends.'[10]
More recently Jean Rostand has said, in an interview about
Jacques Monod's *Le Hasard et la Nécessité*: 'In my opinion,
however much I admire this book, it does not present any new
philosophy . . . He seems to consider that the small changes
that occur in the nucleic acids have been sufficient to achieve
the whole of evolution from the first living creatures down to
man. I myself think that some mechanisms exist of which we
are as yet unaware. And let me make it clear that in saying
this I am prompted by no underlying spiritualist and certainly
no religious motive. Teilhard de Chardin would have answered
you by saying: evolution is conducted by God Who will
lead it to the omega . . . I simply have a feeling that
something is missing in the interpreting mechanisms, something that is almost certainly of a physical or chemical
nature . . .'[11]

But the atheism of Sartre, the stoicism of Rostand, the
doubters of the perfect rationality of the world, are best
answered by the greatest scientific genius since Newton—Einstein. This is what he says: 'The infinite comprises all and
controls all things . . . The structure of a system is the work
of reason . . . The empirical data and their mutual relationships
must find their representation in the conclusion of the design.
It is the possibility of their representation which confers its
only value and its only justification on the whole system and on
the concepts and principles which form its basis. This apart,
these concepts and these principles are free inventions of the
human intellect, which cannot be justified either by the nature
of this intellect or by any form of *a priori*.'[12] And: 'I am convinced that one can discover, thanks to purely mathematical
constructions, the concepts and the laws linked one with the
other, which give the key to natural phenomena . . . No doubt,

experience remains the only criterion of the usefulness of a mathematical construction; but the creative principle resides in mathematics. In a certain sense, I hold it as true that pure thought is capable of apprehending the real, as the ancients have dreamt that it was so.'[18] One could not be more Platonist, more convinced of the importance of pure thought, mind, or imagination in apprehending or recognizing the real, which is the permanent. 'Progressively,' Einstein continues, 'I came to the conclusion that it was impossible to discover true laws by starting from construction from known facts.' Yet, that is what some scientists try to do, and with unforeseen results, particularly when they move from physics to metaphysics, from the particular to the general. In reply to the critics of his theory of relativity, Einstein says: 'The value of a theory does not rest upon its verification of small effects, but in a great simplification of the basis of physics as a whole', and he goes on: 'To understand why Nature is thus and not otherwise; such is for a scientific mind the highest satisfaction . . . One feels that God Himself could not have organized these relations otherwise than what they are in fact, any more than it could be in His power to turn the figure 4 into a prime number . . . This is the Promethean element of scientific experience . . . it is, if I may say so, the religious basis of the scientific effort.' 'Einstein', said Max Born, 'had faith in the power of reason to discover the laws according to which God has constructed the universe.' Planck, like Einstein, believed in causality and in the rational order of the world, and they believed that the physical world had a physical reality in space and time which was independent from man. 'There is a real world', said Planck, 'which exists independently of man's act of knowledge, and the real external world is not knowable directly.' Einstein also posited 'the existence of a real universe which liberates the universe from the thinking and apprehending subject. The positivists think that they can do without it; this seems to me an illusion, unless they want to renounce thought itself.' Thought is therefore only possible if one posits the existence of a true reality, free from the thinking subject; we are back to Plato with his ideal world which was also the real, and mind to apprehend it.

The notion of the absurd, so widely entertained in our time, is either a relative, idealistic notion or, if it is an absolute, it necessarily predicates the total incompetence of the one who pronounces about it, since the one who does so is part of it. For if there is only the absurd, then the absurd is all, including the subject who predicates it. If the absurd is a relative notion, then the subject who posits it must not only be conscious of perfect rationality and order, but also situate the absurd within the structure of order and rationality which must obviously be the whole, or at least the dominant aspect of human life, to which the absurd belongs. If the absurd were dominant, it would be most unlikely that the greatest geniuses, the Greek artists, Shakespeare, Dante and others, should not have stressed this aspect of life, the absurd, instead of the rationality, the growth of human experience, and order. This would of course be a denial of the universality of the strength of their genius which, if it had concentrated on purely sectional and limited aspects of the life of man—absurdity being one of them—to the detriment of the whole, or a section not integrated in the whole, could only have been very limited in scope and significance; and of course, it is not. Whatever the significant character in any one of the works of these great geniuses does, he is always conscious that his freedom and behaviour are part of the divine or universal rationality and justice which, in the end, must prevail, and whose triumph is always part of the final impression conveyed by these works. Lear's decision to renounce his throne is not absurd; it is unexplained, but it is neither unmotivated nor inhuman. Power can tire, or one may want to test the will of those who support it, or even require reassurances. Lear's daughters' behaviour is not absurd, but unnatural, that is to say irrational, purely instinctive and self-centred.

Being can neither be reconciled with any notion of a totally absurd creation, nor leave room for choice, because choice implies separation between Being and the various entities from which it would choose, and varying degrees of knowledge of those aspects of creativity. This is not possible, for Being's knowledge is neither graded nor gradual, it is constantly perfect at the level of essences. Being is self-knowing both at the level of essence and at the level of actualization, but the actualization is the necessary realization of Being, that is to say of what is pure Being shorn from non-Being. Being is both transcendent and immanent. It is transcendent in the sense that its reality informs creation and the cosmos; it is immanent in the sense that it informs the actualization of some of the virtualities which pertain to being. These virtualities are actualized, not through a continuous particular will or guiding force, but according to their essences which are more or less sufficient for total or partial actualization. Thus some actualizations succeed and others fail, for there are many virtualities which are wanting in essence and therefore are not actualized.

There is order, but it is not the order of a mobile placed in a groove from which it cannot swerve and in which it cannot stop. It is the order of a general purpose which is the actualization of Being, the order of a river which necessarily flows downward, but the waters of which can overflow its banks, spread out over marshy ground and even get lost in sandy soil. There is order along a broad direction, with the possibility of trial and error. Some small streams become rivers, which connect with still greater rivers and reach the sea. Others start, but get lost on the way, in the same way as in a forest, many seeds fall to the ground, but only a few begin to grow, and among these few many will stop half-way because they are crushed by other plants, by the elements or by other forces. It is the same with the various virtualities of Being. Many are eliminated, but the orientation of Being and its order of unfolding are unperturbed and, in fact, the force which activates this order presides over the elimination of the various useless virtualities and only fosters those which are truly part of the essence of positive actualization. Being is aware, at any time, of all the virtualities of any substance or essence. Each essence, substance or form is a whole with its special structural connections with the structure of the universe, and with virtualities and inner laws for its actualization. This essence or substance is part of and is connected with the essence of Being, and therefore part of the unfolding of Being.

Each essence actualizes perfectly or partially a given aspect of essential, eternal truth, and it retains the knowledge or self-awareness of this truth, as part of the true reality of Being. This self-awareness necessarily re-cognizes, through Being, the self-awareness of the parts of the truth which are close to, or have affinities with itself, and are therefore part of the same awareness, or of an awareness which is close to it, within Being. Each individuated essence contains all the virtualities which may or may not be actualized in the contingent world. But the fact that nothing can happen which is not inherent to the essence of the individuation, does not mean that there is an iron order which foretells or precludes any swerving, hesitations, or any contingent, superficial intervention. That the end is in the beginning, that God, or Being, can see the way in which every essence or substance will be actualized, does not mean that essence or substance, actualizing itself in Time, has only one single, uniform way of doing so, within a strictly enforced and fully determining fate. God or Being can see or know the end or finality of every essence, but the individuated essence does not know its end until it has achieved it, and therefore it follows a pattern of trial and error towards its finality which is the final discovery of itself through actualization.

The fact that certain possibilities and virtualities are rejected does not mean that they could not come to exist, or that it was impossible for them to be actualized. It means that what has been actualized was neither, strictly speaking, absolutely necessary, nor ineluctably determined. Nevertheless the fact that it has been actualized proves that there were in it the virtualities which corresponded best to the essence which was seeking its perfection through actualization. So that, in the end, one is faced with the fact that there is an appearance of free-will, of interplay of chance and determinism, within the context of the contingent world, but this is merely an appearance, from the point of view of transcendence or of true knowledge of the exact strength of the component elements of any given essence, for it is the inner composition of these elements which determines the way its possibilities and virtualities will reach or not reach actualization.

Every essence not only includes the virtualities of its actualization, but is related both to other essences by continuous possibilities and virtualities which make interaction and structural relations with other essences possible, and to Being as part of an overall pattern, which determines the structural affinities and finality of all individuated essences. The fact that individuated essences are both finite in their existential actualizations, and infinite in as far as they achieve the perfection of their truth, is what relates them to Being. This means that an individuated essence could be in conflict with other individuated essences on the contingent plane, and remain incomplete, and therefore unable to harmonize with the essential structure to which it is destined, though it might be able to make a partial or even a negative contribution to it. But this contribution, whatever it is, is nevertheless part of Being's purpose, to reach absolute self-knowledge through actualization which is the only way of separating being from non-being. The essence of any individuation contains the forms or ideas of things which enable it to re-cognize these things, or rather the truth of these things. Without these forms or ideas as parts of essence, there would be no means of apprehending the truth of their phenomenal appearance.

The world is perceived according to the ideas and forms that we possess of it. This does not mean that the phenomenal world only exists through the perceiving subject, in Berkeleyan fashion; it means that the perceiving subject possesses, in himself as part of his essence, or rather, every individual possesses in varying degrees, the forms, the ideas which will enable him to apprehend the truth of certain things. Nor is it a question of remembering past lives. It is a question of forms, of individuated essences being the same as, or being analogous in structure to, the forms of the phenomenal world—all parts of the same source, therefore, part of Being.

5

Evil and Suffering

Soyez béni, mon Dieu, qui donnez la souffrance
Comme un divin remède à nos impuretés.

BAUDELAIRE

There are here two problems which have exercised man's mind through the ages. There is, first, the one concerning the fact that the force of any individuated essence determines, or seems to determine, the existential shape which the individuation will have. This would seem to submit all aspects of life to a very rigid determinism; yet it is not so, for, as explained previously, the will to exist operating within a large number of virtualities and possibilities is not necessarily compelled to choose one single given virtuality, though it obviously chooses between what is absolutely best and what is possible. One must bear in mind the fact that the best is not necessarily always possible and in all places. That would be to say that one single essence unfolding by itself, on its own, would necessarily choose the best of all its possible existential shapes, provided it were equipped with all the possibilities from which to choose its perfection. But one must not forget that possibilities necessarily imply impossibilities, and perfection implies imperfection. Still, it is possible to think (if this concept were possible, which it is not) that one essence in isolation would achieve its best possible actualization, purely according to its own form. But essences always operate with other individuated essences, each seeking actualization, therefore one has to take into account not only the inherent contradictions existing in every individuated essence, but also the contradictions which every individuated essence constitutes for the others. This, of course, increases the margin of uncertainty about the actualization of certain possibilities, without in any way being able to alter the fundamental relationship of all individuated essences to Being.

Being knows what will be, or rather, this is not the way to put it, for the expression 'what will be' applied to Being is meaningless. Being simply is, and is one and eternally the same, in the sense that the becoming of Being through existence and Time is merely a notion apprehended as extension by the finite mind, while it is apprehended as an eternalized instant by Being itself. Therefore if Being knows what will be through Time, whatever is through Time is from the point of view of Being ineluctable and necessary, and this is truly so, for actualization is either absolutely necessary to its becoming, or it is the prey of chance and individuated free will. That would not be Being, but chaos, from which Being would be supposed to emerge and to make itself.

Being itself has obviously freely chosen what it is, but 'freely' here can only be equated with 'necessarily', for Being, all knowing, could only choose the best and nothing else. Freedom is therefore only an appearance in the finite world of Time—the domain of the actualization of the infinite possibilities of essence. These possibilities are infinite for man's mind, but they are not so for Being which knows them all, including their negative and positive aspects. This being so, it means that the evil behaviour of Judas was as much a revelation to his fellow apostles and to his time, as Hitler's evil behaviour was to the twentieth century. But neither sample of evil behaviour could be said to be a revelation to Being, which knew, at the level of essence, what these actualizations would be. Judas was part of the same timeless necessity which presided over Christ's incarnation, and this goes back to creation itself and to the very first man, for without creation which is finite, and therefore imperfect, there could not have been any ignorance or any need to enlighten men about the true way to perfection, or any other way for Being to know itself through His incarnation and death in Time. Death, the disintegration of an organic in-dividuation, would have been unknown to Being except at the level of essence, that is to say except as virtuality, that is to say as part of a state of perpetual equilibrium between Being and non-Being, transparent, bottomless, and reflecting abso-lutely nothing—a pure diamond or a perfect void, without the slightest cloud or sound—a perfection of a kind, certainly, but a perfection which could not possibly know itself, since noth-ing can only reflect nothing. Thence the need to know itself through extension, actualization and the impurities and imper-fections of creation which, as previously mentioned, constantly and endlessly sieves being from non-being.

This continuous process of sieving being from non-being necessarily entails the actualization of the positive and the negative, and of what one calls in human terms the good and the bad. The process, part of the necessity and knowledge of Being, takes place within the perspective of Being, and is a purely natural and totally non-anthropomorphous process. The epithets good and bad, or good and evil, have absolutely no meaning within it. These actions and transformations are what is absolutely necessary and ineluctable in the actualization of Being, which cannot be implicated in human terminology, or weighed by human tribunals and saddled with human responsi-bilities. These things are, and their final meaning, place and necessity in the order of Being eludes the finite mind, and should not be used as a means to shift man's own responsibili-ties on to the Absolute, or to blame it for the 'evil' of mankind. Transcendence cannot be assessed by the finite, and it is only involved in the finite through immanence. Evil, crime and other failings are part of the ways of men and cannot be given meta-physical roots, or sanctions, except in as far as they reflect a loss of sense of direction, or a lack of true relationship between man and man—something which implies a lack of true relation-ship with Being. To say that Evil is necessarily part of the actualization of essence in Time neither implicates nor involves the responsibility of Being. One has therefore to judge evil, the good and the bad, on the human plane and simply see what one can make of them, without any metaphysical implications, or notions of original sin.

The Dostoyevskian notion that without God everything is permitted is, to my mind, erroneous on many counts. The age-old dilemma concerning the impossibility of reconciling God's omnipotence and omniscience with evil obviously rests upon a rather superficial notion of God as an all-controlling, all-directing and supervising power. It is a notion that reduces God either to a pantheistic divinity or to an ever-proliferating Manichean entity producing as many angels or demons as there are individuals on earth or on any inhabited planets in the universe. This is not therefore the notion of God as the substance or informing force of life, but of God as an absolute dictator or ever-present, ever-interfering Big Brother. It is a notion that can be entertained not on the plane of reason but only on the plane of simplified, utilitarian theology, or on that of animism, as in the case of primitive societies. The only rational notion of God which makes possible some kind of freedom, the nature of which will be briefly examined later, is that of God as informing being in Time, its essence realizing itself to the best of its positive potentialities, and by so doing, contributing through such realizations or actualizations to the knowledge of being and to the completion of the self-knowledge and perfection of Being. Plato, in the *Thaetetus*, had already suggested that 'men participate in the knowledge of God's eternity, through contemplation'.

It is not possible to conceive of Being as constantly intervening to modify the evolution and the actualizations of individuated essence. This would be contrary to the notion of the ideally perfect knowledge possessed by Being, which would thus be constantly altered by contingencies instead of constantly accommodating or assimilating them to fit the self-contained, immutable finality of the essence which informs individuated being and connects it with Being. On the biological plane it would mean that life is either constantly tossed about by chance mutations due to all sorts of causes, or has to be guided by a force which must be forever on the look-out to keep it, through constant interventions, on its pre-set track; while, on the contrary, life unfolds according to the affinities and properties of the elements which compose the chemical aggregates and the biological molecules, the self-caused finality of which is always able to adapt any contingent intervention to the inner logic and purpose of an evolutionary creation. On the metaphysical plane, evolution takes place according to the appetites and affinities of the individuated essences, and according to their positive virtualities for full being, or their lack of positive virtualities which are annihilated into nothingness, which, on the plane of history and organized social life, corresponds to the basic notion of Evil. Evil is therefore a lack of being, that is to say an incapacity, due to certain limitations of individuated essence, to become fully conscious of true being, part of Being.

An existent may, owing to such limitations, think or believe that goodness consists entirely in satisfying his desires and longings, irrespective of the effect that such an attitude or such behaviour may have on others; he may believe that his freedom consists in the fulfilment of his own self-interests and desires; yet, in fact, this is not fulfilment, but slavery as far as he is concerned, and it is oppression and tyranny as far as his relations with others are concerned. It is obvious that the existent who behaves according to such rules lacks sufficient positive essence to enable him to transcend his own limitations and self-interest, and to connect with the true essence of Being, which necessarily posits goodness as part of its perfection. Goodness consists not in trying to achieve the fulfilment of one's own desires—something which is in fact non-fulfilment and non-being—but the fulfilment of all the aspects of life which tend to reunite being with Being. This can only be done by endeavouring to liberate the existent from the servitude of his self-centred appetites, which are far more tyrannical than any external tyranny, and by his thinking and behaving in such a way that whatever he does or thinks could always be universalized without causing any suffering or any diminution of being to other existents.

This is the only way to achieve freedom, or to make freedom possible, and this freedom rests upon the Kantian and Christian notion of making it possible for the individual self to conform to the Law, or to merge into true being. In order to do that, the individual self, whatever the limitations of his essence, must try to know what true being really is. The innate limitations of individuated essence obviously connect with the intractable problem of responsibility for evil in society, and with the various ways of dealing with it. My view is that innate limitations of essence do not preclude either attempts to acquire or to develop, through individual effort and through support from others, a vague consciousness of evil, or the adoption by society of institutions which minister to these failings and needs, and also of measures to prevent or even to make impossible the repetition of certain manifestations of evil once they have taken place. These efforts to live with evil ought to be carried out in a spirit of compassion and brotherhood towards those who are less endowed than others, and a desire by those who know the truth and the experience of freedom to help as much as possible those who, through essential limitations, are deprived of them.

The New Testament says: 'Ye shall know the truth, and the truth shall make you free.' To know the truth is to know the true nature of being, and in the end, freedom is not a question of examining and weighing various hypothetical alternatives as if they were objects laid out upon an imaginary table, but of trying to discover, out of the various forces pressing confusedly upon the mind and the heart, the light which could guide one to an apprehension of the true nature of being. Once this apprehension has been achieved, either through conscious efforts and a shedding of egotistical impediments, or through unexpected moments of surrender and illumination, enlightenment and freedom may come.

Man's freedom does not depend on the existence or non-existence of God as a rewarding or chastising hand; it depends on his capacity to discover through his conscience, which is the light that connects him with Being, what he ought to think or do in order to harmonize his life so as to contribute to the maximum goodness and to the spiritual well-being of mankind through the actualizations of all the positive virtualities of being, and the rejection and relegation into non-being of what is fit neither for being nor for Being, neither for Time nor for Eternity, for in the end it is through Time that Eternity makes itself. One must cease trying to enclose God in the all too facile and impossible dilemma between omnipotence and guilt, and a limitation of power fit only for Manicheism or polytheism. These are purely anthropomorphic notions which cannot be applied to Being, and it is because most theologies have personalized God that they have never been able to solve the problem of evil. Being certainly knows everything as essence, but knowledge as essence is not the same thing as knowledge through existence, or through incarnation and the continuous activity of the Holy Spirit. Knowledge as essence is ideally perfect, since it is knowledge of knowledge, and it is by definition unaware of any flaws, imperfections or absences, which can only reveal themselves through individuations which actualize in Time all the positive virtualities of their essence, and thus contribute through objectification to the absolute self-knowledge and perfection of Being.

If man cannot shift his moral responsibility on to a present or absent God, he can even less base his morality on so-called objective knowledge acquired through science. The knowledge of true being, which is the basis of freedom and morality, has very little to do with the perceptual, physical, biological or sociological knowledge which is advocated as a possible basis of the ethics of knowledge by some scientists. This notion is, in principle, as subjective and as dogmatic as any of those aspects of religious belief which scientists reject as meaningless and unverifiable. To be sure, objectivity is only a dream, and even the greatest living philosopher of science, Karl Popper, says

practically as much in his book, *Conjectures and Refutations*.
Scientific knowledge, as a whole, is neither ethical nor un-
ethical; it is neutral; like Aesop's tongue, it depends upon the
use one puts it to—it can be good, and it can be bad. Scientific
knowledge certainly can confer material power upon those who
possess it or produce it, but it does not confer any spiritual
power whatsoever. On the plane of the spirit, St Francis, shorn
of all his material possessions, yet overflowing with hope, love
and compassion for his fellow-beings, or Socrates, ready to die
for his faith in truth and immortality, are far more powerful
and of greater import for mankind than Von Braun, maker of
rockets that may go to the moon or be used as terrifying instruments of destruction. In bacteriologists like Pasteur or
Fleming there is only good, but it is a different problem to have
brilliant bacteriologists all over the world devoting (so they
think) their knowledge to the preparation of the impossibility
of bacteriological warfare. This kind of patriotic sophistry,
which ought to be alien to the true scientific spirit, is at the
mercy of any apprentice sorcerer who, like Hitler, could compel them or prevail upon them to put the products of their
knowledge to the service of his destructive power. Yet perhaps
the worst feature of this dream of an ethics of knowledge is
that this kind of knowledge could only be the privilege of the
few—the scientists—who would necessarily be the priests of
the new morality.

The notion that one could make of so-called objective,
scientific knowledge the basis of ethics is so fraught with
difficulties that even Professor Monod, one of its best-known
sponsors, finds it difficult to avoid some self-contradiction. For
instance, he says: 'The very definition of true knowledge rests,
in the last analysis, on a postulate which belongs to ethics.'[1]
On the next page he says: 'Knowledge in itself excludes any
kind of value judgments (except those which have an epistemological value), while ethics which is by nature non-objective is
for ever excluded from the field of knowledge.'[2] The second
statement is intrinsically more acceptable than the first, but it

would seem rather to contradict the first. Indeed, knowledge is above all concerned with truth and not with ethical values; and besides, it is difficult to see how one could assess the value of the ethical postulate which is the basis of knowledge, since knowledge itself is supposed to be, as previously stated, the basis of ethics. We are back to the chicken and the egg, and we are in the end faced with the subjective choice of a basic value which rests not on knowledge but on belief.

Truth as a universal is, of course, an ethical value as much as beauty and goodness; but with the word 'universal' we are in the domain of philosophy and not the domain of science. We are in the domain of Keats's 'Beauty is truth, truth beauty', where Dostoyevsky's wish that 'one day beauty might save the world' might come true. In this domain, for those who do not base ethics on the search for the true being as perfect goodness, or on the Kantian categorical imperative, the problem consists in distinguishing the true from the false and the good from the bad, either according to purely human standards or by giving them a transcendental substratum, which has, in various forms, always been part of man's perennial thought. Although he describes man as 'alone in the indifferent immensity of the universe from which he has emerged by chance',[3] Professor Monod cannot define the notion of the ethics of knowledge without bringing in the notion of transcendence: 'The ethics of knowledge . . . implies a transcendent value— true knowledge—and proposes to man not to make use of it, but henceforth, through a deliberate and conscious choice, to serve it. It is, however, also a humanism, for it respects in man the creator and the depository of this transcendence.'[4] So man, having originated from blind, absolute chance—the basis of evolution—creates transcendence or transcendental values. Therefore, although there is no room for God or transcendence, there is obviously room for a chosen few (scientists or others) who know what true knowledge is, and who are the depositories of transcendental values and recondite axioms which can endlessly tease the layman's imagination. Take, for instance, this one: 'The ethics of knowledge is equally, in a certain sense, knowledge of ethics.'[5] A marvellous sentence, glimmering at the dark entrance of the temple of the divinity called knowledge; mysterious like the sphinx's smile, a closed circle like the image of the Egyptian serpent that bites its own tail! But it is difficult to know the exact nature of the ethics here suggested, for the knowledge upon which it is based excludes, in principle, the subjective aspects of human life which—from love of mankind and love of beauty to the questionings and dreams about man's origins, nature and finality—cannot be encompassed by science. The duty to know, in the sense of knowing history, sociology and the laws of nature, etc., obviously cannot constitute an ethics of knowledge. The only knowledge basic to ethics is the knowledge of true being or true love, which is the substance or the force which holds all men together in an I-and-thou relationship which extends to and embraces the divinity.

The notion that existence is a manifestation of Being, and therefore dependent upon its laws, neither diminishes the role of the human personality nor reduces it to that of a robot in a deterministic, predictable world. As previously pointed out, determinism at the existential level is no more predictable than free will. It simply means that everything in creation is inherently and coherently related to causes, part of the becoming of Being, instead of being self-caused as free will ought, in principle, to be. Such a notion cannot be seriously entertained either as a metaphysical or, least of all, as a phenomenal notion. The notion of man choosing his decisions and through them making himself, in a constant state of Promethean defiance of causal limitations or ontological fears, is a noble one, but it is, alas, difficult to uphold. In fact, unless the notion of man's freedom is removed from this idealistic, abstract plane and brought down to the plane of exact knowledge of the existential, social conventions, laws and regulations, and put together with an accurate self-knowledge or consciousness of the workings of man's mind and emotions, it remains only a verbal game and an illusion much misused by priests and autocrats in order to control or to terrify their fellow beings.

It can reasonably be argued that in fact we do not make our choices, for we cannot separate the choosing *I* from the chosen attitude or decision; we cannot, indeed, turn the hypothetical choosing *I* into an ever newly minted entity as virgin of any marks or imprints of time and life as the primal dawn. The dice are loaded, the *I* is trailing with it a whole nexus of causal entanglements with past events and future hopes which make any truly free choice impossible. All that the choosing *I* can do is not to choose but to know what its choices are, and through its choices and actions to know what it truly is. The attitudes or alternatives towards which we seem to be directing our attention—that is to say, the attention of an hypothetical entity called the *I*—are those which are uppermost in our minds as dominant yet unrevealed elements of our psyche.

Our so-called choices are in fact the emergence of these elements into the light of consciousness, with which they fuse to become the unfolding pattern of our personality. This personality is not curtailed by being looked upon as causally connected with the becoming of Being. A morality which rests upon the true knowledge of being and upon the categorical duty to bring about the actualization of God's will as universal goodness and love, precludes egoism or retributory attitudes towards human failings, and advocates reformatory and preventive measures which are not very different from those proposed by the believers in free will. Such a morality is based upon the concept that if men are normal, they are rational, and as such it is their duty and responsibility to endeavour to conform to the logos or reason which is God's will.

God has written neither the exact meaning nor the end of creation in creation itself; but the essence which informs creation, which compels it to be what it is, is a purposive energy, and as such it contains the virtualities of its unfolding and end. If man, according to Marxism, makes history, and it is true that he does, he makes it, not as if he were a self-created entity, continuously possessed with free-will, but as part and parcel of a continuously evolving creation, that is to say as part of a whole which has a purpose of which man is part, and which he progressively reveals. Creation makes itself and reveals itself progressively according to various successive stages of development, and according to the forces and the places involved. These developments, though not predetermined in the sense that an omnipotent power has decided in advance what will take place, are nevertheless determined by, or rather caused by, the state of the forces or elements which compose them. Some forces may appear as strong and uppermost at certain moments, and in certain places; some beliefs may appear as firmly held and widespread, and yet they may not be the dominant element of the evolutive process of creation; therefore they will soon be absorbed in others, or discarded, and they will not play much of a part in the process of historical evolution.

In spite of the fact that it is rotten to the core, a tree may look as if it were set to live for centuries; yet it will collapse at the first storm. The tree could not know of its coming fall, although man could discover it if he happened to examine it. Nothing existing can know the scope and span of essence. Only essence itself could have this knowledge, and essence can only know itself through existence, therefore essence itself does not know its final form, since essence is in itself an orientation towards a plenitude which it seeks to achieve and know through existence. Only Being, as entity separated from essence at work in creation, could know the finality of essence and creation; but that would mean conceiving of Being as the unmoved mover of creation, made of chaos or non-Being, a notion which is untenable, for it would make Being finite, and therefore an object and not the subject of becoming.

Evil and suffering are part of becoming; they are so, not as manifestations of motivated will, but as part of the process of change, the finality of which is spirit. Evil lies in the naturally destructive character of things, each struggling for the realiza-

F

tion of its own essence. The phenomenal ascendancy and apparent importance of a given thing or object is no indication of its true essential worth. A field of completely scentless flowers might, from the point of view of worth, be far less valuable than a single rose. A given aspect of social life might seem important, and yet be totally valueless and insignificant, while another aspect, not showing any striking signs of importance at the phenomenal level, might have deep roots which profoundly affect life and which will go on affecting and transforming life increasingly in the future. Here lies the difference between fashion and truth.

Evil is part of the conflict of opposites, unavoidable and contingent to the final aim of the lastingness and permanence of good. Evil is negative, therefore it will be eliminated from the permanent aim of Being, which is totally positive. But the negative is part of the necessary growth of good and unfolding of creativity. Evil is suffering and deprivation of life by beings who, by definition, cannot give back life; therefore killing, whatever form it may take, legal, patriotic, or otherwise, is always, in varying degrees, evil. To suffer evil is the only way to defeat it. Suffering, whether redemptory or as means of purgation, is part of life and has great heuristic value, but its redemptory aspect cannot be accepted as being part of Christ's mission on earth. Suffering can, no doubt, be enlightening; yet it must not be overwhelming, and it is nevertheless part of the evil which plagues mankind. Evil being a necessary part of finitude, it is unthinkable that Christ should have come to earth to redeem evil through suffering and death. Suffering, as the Book of Job proves, can be a means of opening up and raising the individual to the knowledge and the apprehension of God and higher truth. But, in order to do that, God had to allow Satan to tempt Job. Suffering is a means of truly understanding and sharing in the plight of the human condition.

St Augustine's *etiam peccata* certainly indicates that he sees evil as a means to learn and to reach the supreme good. It stands to reason that evil is part of immanence and part of the imperfection of beings, which cannot by definition possess the perfection of Being. Plato said: 'Nobody is evil of his own free will.' Will is a matter of knowledge, that is to say, of knowing what one wants to do. The knowledge of what one wants to do is the prerequisite of the will to act. The will, that is to say the motive force of action, is the knowledge of the action which one wishes to perform. Will does not mediate between the pros and cons and the varied aspects of a given problem, weighing one against the other. Will is the motive for acting emerging as the dominant aspect of a given situation, the other aspects being so weak as to be eliminated by this prominent aspect which motivates the individual to act.

The robber knows what he wants, and the way to obtain it, but his consciousness does not include in this knowledge, except in a soon-discarded or inchoate form, the moral values of his action, and the various risks he might incur; at least it does not include them in a way which could be strong enough to eliminate the other aspects of his projected action and consequently preclude it. Nobody willingly causes suffering unless he is a sadist, that is to say unless he does so as part of the negative aspect and imperfection of his essence. Yet numerous social systems of mankind cause evil, and ignore suffering, and it must be said that for too long religion has partly comforted itself with the thought that those who suffer on earth will be redeemed and rewarded in Heaven. Suffering transcended can be, and is, ennobling and a credit to man in his puny fight against his fate and against his limitations; but long, protracted suffering, in abjection and in conditions which make it impossible for man to rise above it, is degrading and unworthy of the human condition, and certainly unworthy of transcendence, for those who believe that transcendence could have any part whatsoever in it.

Evil and suffering are part of the necessary harmony of pure Being which can only be reached through the resolution of opposites and of the negative aspects of creation. Whitehead writes in *Religion and the Modern World*: 'What is the way of value is the attainment of life. And it cannot find such value till it has changed its individual claim with that of the objective universe. Religion is world's loyalty."[6] This means that the individual must assume responsibility towards others and the world, and must merge his individuality with the universal or divine order, for, as Dante put it, only *in sua voluntade e nostra pace*. This also rejoins the categorical imperative of Kant; it merges the individual interest in the general good, and the logos or God is the mediating element through which one must pass in order to go from the individual to the universal. This transformation cannot take place in any other way. To pass from the individual to the universal and perennial, a mediator, a point of reference, is necessary. In that respect, the incarnation is the crux, the burning point of reference and the means by which it is possible to ascertain the value which every individuation and actualization has in relation to Being and Eternity. Religion gives man what nothing else can give him— a perspective of events and a pattern to follow, so as to reach the universal through the present and existence.

6

Christ and Socrates

In our anthropomorphic age, in which God has been proclaimed dead by Nietzsche and Being is 'without reason, without cause and without necessity',[1] man is a 'useless passion' and life is looked upon as absurd. Men, deprived of God, nevertheless 'aspire to be God', would like to know everything, and dismiss what is beyond their knowledge as irrational. They ignore the fact that knowledge is always subjective, limited, relative, and never absolute, for the absolute cannot be known, though it is an intelligible concept of pure reason. God is, by definition, incomprehensible; if He were not so, He would not be God, but a mathematical truth. Besides, from the Hebrews who, in Deuteronomy, told their God that His presence was too terrifying, to the Hindus, the Greeks and others, the absolute or the Divine has always to be mediated through avatars or incarnations. The Socratic moral imperative: 'Know thyself', which echoes Apollo's command, simply means: know thyself as a man among men, know what you are—a finite being who can only reach the supreme truth through death. God took human shape so that men might know His truth through Christ, but His incarnation meant death. Both Socrates and Christ testify to the fact that there cannot be any profound human knowledge or revelation of ontological truth without suffering and death.

Socrates and Christ illustrate, each in his own way, the same crucial need to recognize the fact that man is born for death, that life is necessarily tragic, and that it is through the acceptance of this truth, and not through any crude materialism or superficial notions of absurdity, that man can be filled with concern for the other, who is a brother and not an enemy. Life is tragic, and has always been so, since the dawn of human consciousness which taught man his finitude and his ever-impending death. 'Life is but a tale told by an idiot, full of sound and fury, signifying nothing': this is merely the last cry of a thwarted, ambitious man on the verge of the void, of which he is terrifyingly conscious. Life is King Lear's noble acceptance of blindness, destitution and human sorrows, with the words: 'Ripeness is all.' Life is what blind, heart-wracked Oedipus Colonus describes with his last words: 'In spite of so many trials, my advanced age and the greatness of my soul, make me say that all is well.' 'Tragedy', said Hegel, 'is not only misfortune and suffering, but the satisfaction of the mind. The necessity of what befalls individuals is only made clear when it emerges as absolute reason, which then morally calms the soul thrown into turmoil by the fate of the tragic hero, but finally appeased.' 'In my beginning is my end', said T. S. Eliot. 'In my end is my beginning', said Mary Stuart. We are born to die, and death is a new beginning, a beginning without end.

Socrates and Christ, the one interpreted by Plato, the other by St Paul, form the two basic roots of the tree of Western civilization. Neither of them wrote down what he said to men. They both confined themselves to speech and to action, and there is the vital lesson, the lesson valid for religion as well as for morality—that life is above all action. They were both mis-understood, and they both based the authority of their philoso-phy not on any form of mandarinism, but on the life and the reactions of plain people. Christ was a carpenter and his supporters were humble men, and Socrates tested the truth of his philosophy not on sophists, whom he despised, but on artisans. For Socrates immortality was an adventure, a leap into faith, and not a certainty. That is why, beyond the centuries, he links up with Pascal and Kierkegaard. Christ knew his mis-sion; he was sure of his Father's love and his return to Him, and yet at the last moment he could not help expressing his horror of suffering and death with the words: 'My God, my God, why hast Thou forsaken me?' Did this cry express the existential aspect of the Jewish faith, that is to say a faith in which the body and the present were important, while the Greeks, though they lived with all their senses and worshipped the body while it lasted, looked upon them as unimportant and as a mere reflection of the ideal world? Perhaps. Besides numerous gods and goddesses, Greek thought posits the existence of an abstract mind or idea, which is the universal or the absolute to which phenomenal reality is related and by which it is assessed, or rather given its values. Thought itself is objective, and the absolute mind or Idea pervades the universe as a kind of vast continuum of which all created things, including the gods, are part. The world is nothing else but the absolute idea reflecting itself upon phenomenal reality which is the becoming of the absolute. The absolute and phenomenal reality are connected by *nous* or *logos*. Knowledge is not individual; it can only be real if it is related to the essences or to the idea which knows itself as totality.

Christ's incarnation indicates that the Absolute or Being has to be actualized in order to know itself fully, to be known by its individuations and to enable them to participate in the full accomplishment of its creativity. With the Greeks, the soul must be satisfied not through flights into non-being or Nirvana, as in Hindu philosophy, but in itself, by obeying the laws which preside over the equilibrium of the life of the city and of the cosmos. Heraclitus, the precursor of Plato, conceived of the absolute as process or becoming. Being is therefore the first principle, becoming is the second—the *logos*, the creativity which causes actualization through existence, and thus fulfilment of the essence of Being.

In the world of Socrates, there were the laws—divine and human laws—and gods and goddesses, and ideas (Beauty, Justice, etc.) which were supposed to be eternal and true. With Socrates, truth can no longer be accepted as a reflection of the absolute; it must be mediated by thought in existence. The tragedy of Socrates is the most moving after that of Christ, or perhaps even more so, for while the rabbis and the Romans might have looked upon Christ as a rebel, an agitator or an impostor, intent upon the destruction of the political and religious order of the day, Socrates preached the necessity of knowing the limitations of true existential reality and the superiority of individual truth over the ossified laws and conventions of the state. Like Christ, Socrates willed his suffering and his death, which he could have avoided by recanting or by going into exile; he accepted them as the only means to reveal to men ultimate truths which connect them with the divine.

The tragic hero must be responsible for his own death. His actions and thoughts must therefore be, within the context of his own limited knowledge, entirely just and ethical. The power which crushes him must also be, within its own terms of reference, just and ethical. The fate of Socrates was not simply his own, but that of the Greece of his time. On the one side there were the established laws, customs, religion and individual freedom of the citizens, all possessing the right to live according to the laws of the city, on the other there were the divine rights of individual conscience, the right to know, to search for the truth, the right to live by the higher standards of reason and, above all, to allow reason its basic prerogative which is to know itself. These rights are today the very basis of scientific thought and consequently of the major developments of Western science and Western technology.

Socrates did not sneer at, laugh at, or despise his judges and opponents; he only tried, by antithetical and ironic questionings, to lead them towards higher truths which they would not or could not apprehend. This type of irony has nothing to do with irony of contrasts, of grotesque exaggeration of the real in order to illuminate an attitude or a feeling. Socrates was, above all, not so much a moralist as an idealist, a kind of incarnation of the good, who believed in the universal good and who wanted to spread it, so that everyone could share in it. The Greeks had no notion of evil, because they had no notion of freedom from fate, the laws or the gods. They had the notion of obedience or disobedience to the laws of the city and to the gods, and the gods themselves conformed to this pattern of alternation between the two, but unfailingly obeyed the law of Fate which represented, in fact, supreme justice.

Evil, or what is called evil, is part of the finitude of man; it implies either lack of consciousness of the nature of true being, or a daemonic essence, the being of which is evil, that is to say a denial of being—something which would be a contradiction in terms. Lack of consciousness of the true reality of things is synonymous with ignorance or lack of knowledge, to which what is called evil can be attributed in the course of the exercise of our freedom which can only be posited at that price. So we can only be 'free', we can only know certain aspects of the truth, through suffering. Yet, if pain and affliction are too great, they are less a source of knowledge than of abasement and dejection beyond the control of the will. At the point of death, Christ was absolutely wracked by physical pain. Socrates was not, at least not in the same violent way, and there lies perhaps the cause of the difference between their last moments, between the agony of Christ and the serenity of Socrates. Christ, God-man, had reached the point when the vital energy which maintains life can bear no more, and that is why he cried out: 'Enough!' Socrates' test was not, until the final end, a physical test, it was a test of the soul. Christ's soul did not endorse and could not endorse his cry of protest, but his vegetative life could stand no more, and so he cried, and his soul separated itself from his vegetative, tortured body, waiting for reunion with it. The sorrow of Christ in his agony was only equalled by that of God, manifested by His silence. Socrates had no sorrow for himself, and there was no god he could address himself to. Christ knew that he was the Son of God, and he was dismayed at what he thought to be his Father's forsaking of him. Socrates knew that the gods would not interfere in human affairs, unless it was for their own interests. The Greek sky was not empty, but it was too busy with the affairs of its godly performers to hear his call. Socrates hoped that his soul would reach the Elysian fields, where it would have been better than that of the gods, for it would have been completely purified of human passions, while the gods' were not. In the Greek world Fate alone was beyond passions, and it dealt with gods and men with equal detachment. The gods could be both harassed and ordered about by Fate, while demi-gods and demi-goddesses had to die in spite of their semi-divine origin. Christ also was born of a mortal, but he had been conceived not in passion, but because God chose to take human shape, for a given purpose.

From the Greeks to St Augustine, Pascal, Kant and Kierkegaard, man has constantly been aware of the necessity of accepting the irrational as part of life. Believing, whatever its form, has never been equated with knowing, but neither can the concept of Being as a subsistent cause of existence be equated with the anthropomorphic notion of continuous guidance and responsibility for whatever happens in it. This is neither biologically nor metaphysically tenable. Being is creativity, and as such it implies a continuous annihilation of possibilities, therefore a continuous process of negation as part of the process of being. Personal suffering, sorrow and death are the normal lot of man, who dreams of the plenitude of Being. But being can only be at the cost of this lack of plenitude which makes room for nothingness. God could neither be guiding us continually, nor telling us constantly whether what we do is right or wrong. That is not possible. Man is only an atom in the cosmos; it is the general pattern of creation that counts, and the pattern can only emerge slowly, through Time which necessarily carries good and evil, knowledge and ignorance, for just as there is no absolute good in life, but only varying degrees of good more or less tainted with evil, in the same way there is not and there cannot be any absolute evil, for this would be total non-being; there can only be evil tempered by good, and in the end separated from good in the Absolute which is totally good.

7

Science and Philosophy

Les grandes pensées viennent du coeur.
VAUVENARGUES

The present ascendancy of science, and the role which it seeks to assume in certain quarters as a guiding authority of modern life, rest upon a misreading or a misrepresentation of history which is not supported by facts. In the light of this misreading, science is considered to be the high water mark of the growth of man, who is supposed to have moved from the mythical through the religious, to the age of science. Science is looked upon both as a kind of novelty in the history of man, and as the headstone of the human pyramid, and as such it has replaced myth, philosophy and religion. Yet science and the scientific attitude are not a three-and-a-half-centuries-old novelty, nor are they possible substitutes for philosophy or for religion.

There is, in fact, a fundamental, irreducible opposition between philosophy and science, between the philosopher and the scientist, excepting, of course, the mathematician who throughout the centuries has often been both, in the same way as some philosophers were also poets, as was the case with Plato or Nietzsche. The great early Greek thinkers—Anaximander, Pythagoras, Thales, Parmenides, Heraclitus, Empedocles—were in varying degrees mathematicians, and also in varying degrees poets, philosophers and founders of religions or of metaphysical systems. On the other hand, the philosophers of imperial Rome, like Seneca or Cicero, were merely didactic moralists, no longer inventing, but merely propounding systems, and upholding the state. The ancient Greek philosophers were, like Da Vinci and Michelangelo who were painters, sculptors, poets, architects and engineers, universal geniuses. The scope and range of their genius enabled them to embrace practically all aspects of human experience. In them the philosophical, the artistic and the scientific spirit were at one. Democritus invented atomic theories which are still more or less valid in our times. One hundred years before Francis Bacon, Da Vinci stated that experimentalism is the only method of scientific knowledge, and fifty years before Copernicus he declared that the earth was a planet, like the moon.

In modern times, great mathematicians like Leibnitz, Newton (who is generally described as a natural philosopher, but he was also a great mathematician since he discovered the infinitesimal calculus at the same time as Leibnitz), Pascal, Whitehead or Bertrand Russell, were also, in varying degrees, philosophers, but it is clear that they would not, strictly speaking, be primarily described as scientists, at least according to the present-day meaning and connotations of this term.

The scientist is above all concerned, not with the workings of pure reason, but with the workings of practical or experimental reason applied to the observations and structures of phenomena. A philosophic system, a philosophy, is on the whole connected with, and fully true only in relation to, the man who created it. Platonism, besides its universal values, is also Plato, just as Hegelianism is also Hegel, and each of these two great systems will only be totally true for men of stature similar to that of those who created them, and who, therefore, can grasp them in their wholeness. These philosophies, like all philosophies, are not only related to their creators, but also to the time and the place where they were born. The philosopher generally starts from himself, *in situ*, and expresses himself and his time and, of course, beyond, according to the scope of his genius. Whether he endeavours to build up an abstract system like Leibnitz, Kant or Hegel, or endeavours to grasp metaphysical truths, in the philosopher-poet style of Plato or Nietzsche, he is always deeply involved in his creations, and he is always basically concerned with the being of Being. The scientist, on the other hand, starts from facts or from hypotheses, which he seeks to verify or to universalize. Philosophic systems cannot be built upon inductions from facts, or deductions from hypotheses; philosophic systems are built up in attempts to rationalize attitudes to life and to the world, and beliefs about the origins and finality of man and about his relationship with the cosmos and with the eternal flux or will-to-being to which he belongs, and which is also the will of Being.

Scientists uncover the truth of the workings of Nature and of the universe, but these discoveries, which increase rational knowledge, cannot become the foundations of an ethical attitude to life, or the sources of metaphysical truths which are basic to life. By metaphysical truths I mean truths which are valid, not because of their physical or mathematical verifiability, but because of their relationship to rational and meaningful experiences of the universe as a whole. Metaphysical truth is, of course, essentially individual, yet it reaches the universal, and it is apprehensible to all those who approach it, not through facts or phenomena as facts, but through phenomena as appearances of a reality which is not reducible to experimental verifiability. Metaphysics does not exclude rationality; it never did, except in the type of dismissive, surface positivism which flourishes in modern times. On the contrary, it makes use of rationality to logically explore and to expound the coherences and relationships of systems which start from intuition and imagination and not from perceptions or from experimentations upon facts.

Modern times have witnessed the increasing rise of science, and with it, attempts to make of it and of the scientific attitude the basis and the source of all mental activities, thus reducing religion, ethics and even aesthetics to essentially scientific criteria. The answer to the death of God, to the sense of loss of direction, to the fear of the unknown or of impending catastrophe, is the modern Shaman—the man of science who, unless he is a man of genius, has put all his trust in what Whitehead has called 'one-eyed reason'. The truly great scientific thinkers—the great pre-Socratic mathematicians like Anaximander, Thales, Pythagoras or Heraclitus, and the great modern mathematicians like Newton, Leibnitz, Pascal, Einstein or Whitehead—necessarily have a metaphysical view of the universe. The scale of their genius and their imagination is such as to enable them to make discoveries so vast that complete and exact verification of every smallest detail is impossible. Owing to the scope of their genius, they can contemplate their discoveries as complete wholes, in space and time, and as the embodiments of the spiritual forces or energies which animate them. If such an eagle-like gaze leaves here and there slight patches unlit or partly unexplored, this does not alter the truth and reality of the whole observed and held together as a coherence by the informing light of the observer.

The average scientist, lacking the necessary range of awareness that would enable him to see himself as part of an all-embracing whole, naturally seeks to universalize his fragmented observations and to make life conform to the criteria of his vision. This vision is, by definition, limited, and generally perceptual, and it disposes its owner to look at the whole world through the prism of his discoveries—in whatever field he may have made them—and to forget or to gloss over the fact that he is generally not very conversant with anything except the field in which he works. The nature of his observations, which require, above all, concentration upon facts in a narrow, circumscribed domain, precludes receptivity, a wide range of interests and the imaginative capacity to reduce contrasted and remote aspects of life in all its forms to great syntheses whose truth and worth are measured, not by the truth or non-truth of a single fragment or part, but by the truth and coherence of the whole to which these elements belong. Neither Newton nor Einstein could have verified completely and exactly all the aspects of the workings of the systems which they discovered; yet, in each case, their explanation of the life of the whole universe was absolutely coherent and relatively true, that is to say true as far as their minds could reach at the moment in time when they made their discoveries.

Einstein's corrections of the Newtonian system carry with them certain aspects which do not quite conform to the overall truth of his own system. In fact, at the infinitesimally small microscopic level there seem to be particles of massless matter which contradict the general, universal laws which apply to the system as a whole. Yet it is evident that the apparent behavioural unpredictabilities of minutely small particles, without mass and with little energy, neither impinge upon nor alter the orderly behaviour of the whole of matter, at the organic or inorganic level. They seem to be, for the moment, the unavoidable irregularities or unpredictabilities caused by the observation which records them, and therefore they might very well not exist at all if there were no observational interference. This strange Gordian knot cannot be unravelled, since the knower not only records, but also necessarily causes the alteration in behaviour which he observes. In the end, therefore, it can only be cut with the sharp edge of belief, and there, it seems, this matter should rest at the moment.

It is impossible to assert either that these irregularities intrinsically exist, or that they are caused by the presence of the observer. The likelihood that the latter alternative might be true is confirmed by the fact that, these very small exceptions apart, the universe seems to be subject in its entirety to the law of cause and effect and to a perfectly rational order. In fact, when it comes to the laws which preside over the structure of the universe and the growth of human kind or of the individual, the consensus of opinion seems to be practically all-embracing and such as to include idealists like Leibnitz, Hegel or Nietzsche, as well as positivists like Augustc Comte. The principle of the necessity of self-caused forces for the maintenance of life, or what Nietzsche called 'the will to power', that is to say the will or force which animates the becoming of Being, makes being possible and also enables it to achieve its best fulfilment, is upheld even by Auguste Comte. 'No legitimate order,' he says, 'can establish itself, nor above all can it last, if it is not fully compatible with progress; no great progress can effectively take place, if it does not finally tend toward the evident consolidation of order.' Now, it is obvious that some of the terms used by the founder of positivism are para-metaphysical terms and that they embody para-metaphysical notions. If, for instance, one replaces the word 'progress' by the word 'becoming' which is true to life, less abstract and also less ambiguous, one obtains a thought which is perfectly valid now and which, through its implication of self-caused finality, reconciles idealism, vitalism and Marxism. As for the word 'order', it can mean only a metaphysical or idealistic order otherwise called 'Being'.

The inference to be drawn from the above is that purely rational knowledge, within the contemporary limitations of the word, is only one aspect of life, and cannot become or be viewed as the whole of it. The antinomy between knowledge and belief, or between knowledge and certainty, outlined by Kant, still remains unresolved, and cannot certainly be resolved in favour of knowledge. Kant said: 'I had to abolish knowledge to make room for belief; metaphysical dogmatism, that is to say the notion that one may progress in metaphysics without submitting to the critique of pure reason, is the true source of every incredulity and revolt against morality.' Men have now ceased paying attention to such distinctions; they want, above all, to know, to know at any cost, and they tend to think that knowing is all, ignoring, of course, the vital question which is: to know what? The modern problem is, as Schopenhauer put it, that 'knowledge must struggle against knowledge', for otherwise it will become a destructive monster—that is to say, true knowledge must struggle against the mere desire to get information. The instinct to know—a very noble instinct—must not be reduced to the apprentice sorcerer's urge to run the risk of unleashing secrets which he does not care to control, or to lift at all costs the lid of Pandora's box, simply in order to know what is in it, without caring at all about the final outcome of such an action. Least of all must knowledge be the urge to worship what is discovered. Knowledge must have an orientation and an aim—not, of course, the kind of aim imposed by the state, as was the case in the notorious Lysenko controversy, but an aim dictated by the highest and noblest ideals of man.

From the Greeks, the founders of knowledge, to the eighteenth-century explosion of limited or atrophied rationalism, knowledge was always meant to contribute to the benefit of a civilization which was based upon religious beliefs. Now, religion has been partly discarded, and even up to a point replaced by science, and civilization itself is put in dire danger by the frenzy of knowing and, through knowing, of acquiring power. Science has freed itself from the misplaced and short-sighted tyranny of religion when religion was all-powerful and, like all unchallengeable authorities, abused its power. But, having freed itself from the tyranny of religion, science is now succumbing in varying degrees, in communist as well as in capitalist countries, to the blighting tyranny of the state— something which is not more praiseworthy than the tyranny of religion. Will religion, slowly and painfully hammered into new shapes and new relationships with man, ever rise from its past errors and mistakes, regain some of its lost importance, and be once more the binding, living element of civilization? Or will new aspects of spirituality, whatever they may be, take its place? Will it be art, as Nietzsche boldly suggested?— 'Science now can only be controlled by art. It is a question of value judgments, relative to information and the multiple aspects of knowledge. This is an immense task which will bring great dignity to any form of art which can accomplish it. It will have to renew everything and, by itself, create life anew! The Greeks have shown us what art could do; without them our beliefs would be utopian . . . It is possible that art might even have the power of creating for itself a religion, of giving birth to a myth. Thus it was with the Greeks.'

In hoping for the rebirth of myth through art, and in insist-

G

ing upon the importance of myth as the expression of the ethos of a people, Nietzsche was merely being faithful to his belief in the importance of the individual and of the national element in the making of history. Before him, Vico had already deplored the death of myth and the ascendancy of the *verum* over the *certum*. Following Pascal's and Locke's differentiation between understanding and belief or assent, he moved further than either in insistence upon the primacy of certainty over Cartesian, abstract, mathematical truth. He also suggested what became more and more evident with the collapse of religion under the growing impact of science in the nineteenth century : that religion was bound to be replaced by spirit. Mankind had, in fact, moved from myth through paternalistic Judaism to Christianity, which, according to Vico, Hegel, Schopenhauer, Nietzsche and artists like Rimbaud and Mallarmé, could only be followed by the dominance of spirit. Whatever one may think of these views of the evolution of history, the fact is that late nineteenth-century art is torn between positivistic naturalism and transcendentalism in all its forms, from the spiritualism of Pierre Leroux, Mme Blavatsky and other magi, to the transcendentalism of Mallarmé, and, later, the absolute subjectivism of Cubism and Surrealism, which marks the final overthrow of reason and the acceptance of the phenomenal world as nothingness, to be ignored and replaced by the inner subjectivity of the artist.

The ancient Greek philosophers, in spite of the fact that they were practically all mathematicians, never equated truth with certainty. They treated metaphysical truths as poetic truths; with them reason and imagination were at one, and reason possessed poetic powers. They therefore approached their gods through poetic imagination, and they pursued at the same time their unquenchable search for verifiable truth; they kept these two notions firmly apart. What we generally call modern times seems to me to be characterized above all by the attempt to reduce the *certum* to the *verum*, and by the progressive elimination of metaphysics. The period described as modern times did not, of course, begin suddenly, at a given moment; it merely became recognizable as such at a given moment. In fact, rationalism, born with the Greeks, revived by the Schoolmen and by Thomas Aquinas's studies of Aristotle, grew steadily throughout the Middle Ages to reach its apex with Francis Bacon and Descartes, who equated truth with mathematical truth. From then on, truth became more and more synonymous with knowledge, and knowledge tended to replace certainty and belief. This has clearly destroyed the equilibrium upon which life is based, for, if it is undeniable that the aim of life is to know, and to reach the absolute, universal knowledge propounded by Hegel and Nietzsche, it is not possible to reduce truth to rational knowledge without excluding or endangering the very certainties which are the basis of the search for truth.

The reduction of certainty to mathematical truth ended in conferring upon knowledge ontological value. For Hegel, knowledge meant greater and greater self-consciousness, progressing towards the emergence of absolute spirit. Kant maintained the distinction between the noumenon and the phenomenon, and between practical and pure reason. Nietzsche, the last of the great metaphysicians, is more on Kant's than on Hegel's side, and he gives to Kant's categories an aspect of his own, which bristles with complexities and difficulties. First, he begins by defining the notion of knowledge as the attempt 'to schematize and to impose upon chaos the order and form necessary to satisfy practical needs'. Chaos is obviously the complexity and flux of life which the mind, through its action upon it, annihilates. The practical needs alluded to are those which have to be met in order to make life possible. Yet, lest one might be tempted to believe that life is governed by purely practical needs and by reason and logic imposing order upon chaos, Nietzsche explains that chaos represents for him the virtualities of life, including human kind in its entirety and materiality, part of the universal flux bent upon becoming. Therefore this complex world cannot be thought out logically and rationally, but only metaphysically, through poetic reason, by the poet-philosopher, who is for Nietzsche the apex of the human pyramid, the philosopher-king of Plato. So he necessarily concludes that: 'Art has greater value than truth, in the sense that art comes closer to the real and to the becoming of life than does fixed, frozen truth.' The practical needs are the needs to maintain life and being, and to meet the continuous flux of life.

The schematization, the ordering which Nietzsche seeks to impose upon chaos, is carried out, of course, not according to utilitarian terms, which he detests, but according to the Kantian principle which allows reason transforming and transmuting power, and also a guiding idea of what the order should be. In this sense, Nietzsche obviously belongs to German idealism; he takes his place beside Hegel, Fichte and Schelling, and he fully anticipates modern subjectivity objectifying itself through the apprehension or schematization of the phenomenal world. Subjectivity defined in these terms excludes the notion of knowledge as apprehension of facts, or of art as representation of phenomenal reality. This kind of subjectivity, nihilistic in the sense that it denies an alienated society, embodies itself in art, and on the whole, from the end of the nineteenth century onwards, art has been a metaphysical concept, representing the highest value of life and implying the power to transpose and transfigure all aspects of life. Art as such fixes an image of the moving, flowing chaos, and thus becomes the appearance or the visible aspect of that chaos which is apprehensible to the senses, so that truth is not the hidden reality of Plato, of Kant or of faith, but the apparent, the becoming, constructed by mind. Truth is faithful to the becoming which is known as appearance or phenomenon. The next step is, of course, to suppress the distinction and difference between the real world and the apparent world, and if one does that, one suppresses at the same time the possibilities of distinction between truth and error, appearance and reality, and one can only concentrate on the subjective, phenomenological character of truth as part of a universal intersubjectivity. Nietzsche, Rimbaud, Mallarmé attempted to do just that. They suppressed, in varying degrees, both the substance and the shadow, and they sought to live in the light of the eternal noon of art, which is neither false nor true to anything but its own shadowless light which is the incandescent, shining and continuously burning subjective. The artistic transcendence of the subjective is the hallmark of late nineteenth- and early twentieth-century art, including both Cubism and Symbolism.

Such an attitude implying the fusion of the true and the certain into transcendental subjectivity was, of course, confined to the few. The bulk of mankind requires other, more accessible canons of truth and certainty, yet these canons cannot be provided by replacing one by the other, as a certain type of present-day, widespread scientism would like to have it. They can only be provided by the acceptance of the undeniable duality of human life and human thought, in all their aspects; and this duality must be maintained and not reduced to a single form of knowledge or truth, for truth requires a margin or a possibility of error, a fringe or a shadow, shaped by certainties. This belief is best summed up by Nietzsche: 'Truth is a kind of error, without which a certain kind of living being could not live. The value for life, in the end, decides.' Truth is both error and truth at the same time. It both fixes and assimilates chaos, and by so doing, of course, it makes chaos and nothingness part of life, itself part of the totality of Being.

Life is and continues to be; that is a fact; and one cannot conceive of its being and continuing to be as a result of chance, accidents or random forces which could miraculously organize themselves into the most complex, unimaginable order. Life is animated by forces or by a will-to-being and -to-maintain-being which make it possible for Being progressively to know itself. Growing, expanding knowledge seems to be the *raison d'être*, the very becoming of life, but this is knowledge at the metaphysical level, embracing both the verifiable and the certain; the modern problem is to maintain the equilibrium between the two, and to achieve a vision of the world of which science is part, but which transcends science.

Though art and religion are close in many ways, and although both draw on the noblest aspects of human life and on similar inspirations, they are not interchangeable, and it is not possible to replace one by the other, for the simple reason that the transcendence of art is purely anthropomorphic, while the transcendence of religion is metaphysical, that is to say it enfolds both man and the universe, which possesses its self-caused, ordered, rational will-to-being, transcending the human will. Aesthetics cannot be turned into ethics; art cannot be turned into a basis for morality, though it can greatly contribute to it. Art as morality can only apply to an élite which is purely concerned with self-fulfilment, with a heroic form of living, on the angelic as well as on the daemonic plane, and which is not concerned with good or evil, but with creative, archetypal knowledge, whatever the cost to the searcher or to those who come in contact with him. This attitude consists in looking upon mankind as pabulum for noble, heroic beasts to graze upon, or as compost or manure to grow magnificent flowers in. Men cannot all be Empedocles, requiring a volcano to deify them—and even he, like so many lesser minds, was given the lie by his rejected sandals. If it is not a material aspect which, in the end, denies the divine, there is always some flaw, as far as man is concerned, which prevents him from realizing this impossible, over-ambitious dream. Men must remain men, and as social animals they need some overriding principle based on the practical necessities of life to save them from their natural anthropophagous instincts, or from their latent suicidal tendencies which ever threaten them with the fate of lemmings.

If religion—a renewed form of religion having grown with the centuries, and having understood and adapted itself to the needs of modern man—cannot provide the regulating force and light, I wonder what else can. Yet I am quite certain that, whatever it is, it will not be science. In order that science might be only beneficent to civilization and to mankind, it must be freed from any kind of tyranny whatsoever, as well as from self-worship. It must, in fact, be de-mystified. As Lord Zuckerman put it in one of his admirable lectures: [1] 'Computers may help in assembling and analysing the considerations which have to be taken into account in reaching decisions. They cannot, nor is it likely that they ever will be able to, substitute for human judgment . . . I also hope that the public will never allow the future of mankind to be determined by a new kind of scientific priesthood.' In order to counteract such a danger, the ethical and aesthetic aspects of life must be strengthened so as to restore the balance and to temper the urge to know for knowing's sake, or the tendency to make of knowledge a divinity to replace the one that the world has lost, or an instrument of power in the hands of more and more autocratic, totalitarian states.

Science is neither an ethic, nor an aesthetic, nor a religion. It is a method of acquiring exact, verifiable knowledge of the workings of the natural or phenomenal world. The scientific knowledge thus acquired must have an aim, and it is upon this aim that the life of civilization depends; I mean, of course, the kind of life men lead, and not life as such, for I do not believe that, whatever men may do, they can ever abolish life; they can only alter it—life will go on towards its indeflectable finality.

Civilization's aim cannot be confined to the purely utilitarian task of producing the greatest possible happiness for the greatest possible number of people—futile ambition. First and foremost, happiness is not and cannot be an end in itself. It is the by-product of an attitude to life and of a way of living. Socrates did not die in order to be happy, yet he was happy to die for his beliefs, and, like Christ, he willed his own death in order to prove his truth, which was to know himself and so to decide whether this self was pure or impure, fit for the Acheron or fit for the Empyrean. This is a notion which is also basic to Christianity. Many Christian martyrs have accepted dying for their truth. The day might come when scientists might be prepared to die for the truth of their knowledge, or for the sake of no more Hiroshimas. When that day comes, then science will not become a religion, but it will become fully integrated in civilization, and it will be from then on one of its most beneficent elements. The second point concerning happiness as a possible aim for civilization is that, even if such an aim were accepted, it would be practically impossible to find a common denominator for what could, by and large, be meant by happiness. If this problem were to be solved by being submitted to the opinion of the largest number of people, then there is no doubt that the concept of happiness thus obtained would be something extremely simplified, if not simplistic and shallow. Finally, if the concept of happiness were to be determined by the decision of the greatest number, it would very likely be a materialistic concept.

The aim of civilization cannot therefore be to provide happiness, any more than this can be the aim of individual life. The aim of civilization, the aim of life at the individual as well as at the national level, is to extract or to make possible the realization of what is best and noblest in man or in the society to which he belongs. It is to fulfil to the maximum his potential as will-to-be which informs life at all levels. This fulfilment is both self-caused and controlled by a self-regulating process which is such that life in all its aspects necessarily tends to make full use of all its potentialities and to use them to their utmost. This is neither a theory of automatic progress such as that outlined by Comte, nor a restatement of Hegelian idealism, but something which could be looked upon as a synthesis of Christian, idealistic and materialistic theories of life (whether life is looked upon as pure, yet undeniably orientated matter, or as matter moved by spirit) which all converge upon the belief that the transformation of life takes place as a self-caused, self-regulating process moving towards a form of absolute knowledge or perfect spiritualization.

This aim can only be achieved by unifying the best instincts and ideals of man, and this can only be done by submitting all the aspects of man's life to criteria which have universal value. These criteria can only be ethicoreligious, or at least aesthetic, if aesthetics can be raised to the metaphysical level which it occupied in the multi-religious society of ancient Greece. In that society gods and men dreamed of the same perfection embodied in numbers and ineffable music; then, Keats' words 'Beauty is truth, truth beauty' would have been a reality, and history was ceaselessly transmuted into myth and legend. That age is past and can no more be recaptured than the idyllic, theocratic life of the Middle Ages; though those times can only be described as idyllic if one forgets the substratum of slavery which existed in Greece, and the purely animal life of the villeins in the Middle Ages. Those ages might recur, in different forms of course, if some world-embracing nuclear catastrophe closed the cycle of the present civilization and brought mankind back to the starting-point of new forms of organized life.

This being said, one thing is certain, and it is that these past aesthetic-religious or purely religious criteria of life cannot be scientific criteria and attitudes. To know the way all things work, and what they truly are, is a noble aim, but it cannot be an end in itself. It is only a means to an end which must be part of the meaning and finality which one ascribes to life and civilization and to their relationship with the transcendental forces of which they are part. Crickets take jumps into space without caring about the point where they will land. Men, whatever they do, do not, on the whole, jump or move hoping for the best. They generally have conscious or subconscious projects and aims, informed with the beliefs which they entertain or wish to entertain about life. Science is not, strictly speaking, *sapientia*, and scientists are not quite the sages which some of them would like to be—though it must be noted that the higher they are on the ladder of talent or genius, the more aware they are of their limitations. Scientists are part of life and civilization, the aim of which is not only to know or to verify the structures and workings of the material, perceptual world, but above all to express, that is to say, to bring to consciousness, the true genius which informs it, which gives it its value and is part of the finality of transmuting its component elements into spiritual energy and knowledge. As Baudelaire suggested: 'La vraie civilisation n'est pas dans le gaz, ni dans la vapeur, ni dans les tables tournantes; elle est dans la diminution des traces du péché originel.'

Leaving aside the very debatable question of original sin, which is no longer acceptable in its pristine, theological rigour, it is clear that civilization is not a matter of technological developments or of more and more perfect scientific systems, but of the values which make life worth living, and these values will not emerge from the knowledge acquired through such systems. Nor, above all, can they be obtained by applying to them principles of mathematical verifiability or observational tests which apply to scientific discoveries. These values cannot be objective, scientific discoveries or knowledge. They can only be anthropomorphic discoveries or revelations of what life is, and they are, of course, like all aspects of historical truth, tainted by the world to which they belong, that is to say relative in some of their purely historical aspects, yet perennial in as far as they are part of the flux which carries them forth, and finality which it pursues. Socrates was no less civilized because he had to heat his bath water with a wood fire than those who now heat theirs by turning on an electric switch, and the truth for which he died—the necessity of keeping the soul or conscience pure or untainted by egotistical aims, is no less important now than twenty-five centuries ago. Scientific systems rise and fall, true at one stage, untrue, incomplete, or even obsolete at the next. The permanent values of civilization and of human life never become obsolete, and they can only be transcendental and religious, in a way which does not limit the meaning of these words to any church or any form of organized religion. To believe in the sacredness of human life is a transcendental belief which does not require the existence of a church, though the belief in the existence of Christ or

Buddha gives it a reality, a concreteness which renders the notion more easy to grasp and to hold.

Lest I might be credited with Utopian dreams of a lost Eden or Rousseauesque world in which primitive savages walked and moved surrounded by an aura of goodness which society and science have dispelled, I hasten to state that I firmly believe that the scientific attitude is absolutely inherent in man, that Eden, if Eden there is, lies ahead and not behind, and that whatever has been cannot be undone, erased or recaptured, and, what is more, is not worth recapturing. 'We never step twice into the same stream,' said Heraclitus, and this seems to me as true now as it was in the days of Plato's lecturings at Cape Sunium. As for the scientific attitude, that is to say the curiosity to know, our ancestors, the apes, would still be perched in their trees, and Neanderthal man would still be shivering in his cave, if they had not had the curiosity to explore their environment and to test the secrets of wood and stones. Science is as much a product of the human mind as the search for the truth through myth or through the harmony of lines and colours. Aeschylus and Sophocles, as well as Thales and Pythagoras, were all trying to solve the riddle of the universe, each according to the bent of his mind and sensibility, all of them united in the same reverence for the mystery and the beauty of the natural and supernatural orders. The problem now is that we have lost our reverence for mystery and beauty in a world of greed and lust for notoriety and power. We believe that we know everything, and, new Promethean creatures, we think we are going to live, no longer on earth, but on some kind of Olympus which, of course, will soon be overcrowded and unbearable.

Science, the dream of knowing or of learning, is the most ancient dream of man; it is his original sin, it is his Tower of Babel, his attempt to rise to Heaven, and thus the cause of God's wrath; it is the dream of all the tower-dwellers from Jung to Vigny or Yeats, who have been tempted to snatch a spark of Promethean fire from Heaven. It is also the dream of the cave in which men, heads bent over their fires, tried to extract from them the secret of the philosopher's stone, the source of mystery. But scientific man is not the whole man, and science has never been meant to be the whole of mankind; it is only meant to be a beacon to guide it forward.

Science naturally tends towards dogmatism, on the ground that the truth which it has discovered can be applied to all aspects of life, or, what is even more disquieting, on the ground that only those who possess scientific knowledge can decide about the way this knowledge should be used, or about the means required to maintain and to foster science. The general tone of science is by and large anti-mystical and anti-mythical, and it tends to replace these various aspects of life by so-called scientific criteria of truth, which obliterate whatever cannot be made to conform to purely rationally verifiable principles. This process, unchecked, can result in large-scale utilitarianism.

These various shortcomings of science can only be counteracted, and ultimately disposed of, if science is considered not as a recent aspect of human life which has appeared only in modern times, but as something already present in the cerebral circumvolutions of the first anthropoids and the first man. The fact that the first explanations for the workings of matter or for the mystery of the universe were mythical and religious does not mean that they were anti-scientific. They were, at that moment, the only means man had to answer certain questions and to solve certain mysteries, which could not be dealt with in any other way but through the imagination. Yet the pre-Socratic imagination of Greece gave, through Heraclitus, Leucippus and Democritus, answers about matter and the laws which govern its composition which modern science has neither totally discarded nor totally ignored, for some of their basic principles are still valid today.

As far as Christian civilization is concerned, science could be said to have begun with Aquinas, Roger Bacon, Ockham, Abelard, Duns Scotus, John of Salisbury and others, who were all churchmen and who heralded the experimentalism which was to dominate science. Thomas Aquinas explained Aristotle's philosophy to the Christian world; he was both a rationalist and a believer, and there were many others like him.

Science has, therefore, a very long history, and if it is now either acclaimed by those who see in it the key to the millennium or distrusted by those who see in it only the noxious effects of its discoveries, it is because science has, through some of its representatives (who are never the greatest), tended to assume in our modern society a position which excludes belief and denies real value to any aspect of human life which is not part of its domain, or not answerable to its methods and criteria.

Science discovers, measures and describes the forces and laws of Nature, but it cannot deal with the causality and finality of these laws without passing from the realm of science to that of philosophy. Science finds its own justification in the truth and reality of its results; however, its essence cannot be demonstrated by science, but only by philosophy. Therefore science should never leave its own domain without the awareness that its rules and laws are not transferable in their entirety to other disciplines or other fields of human activity, such as philosophy, ethics or aesthetics. Science can neither replace nor renew philosophy, nor give it a scientific structure so as to render it more efficient or better equipped to discover the truth. This is not possible, for the truth pursued by science is not the truth pursued by philosophy. On the other hand, philosophy can, in as far as it carries a coherent notion of the truth and of the reality of being, inspire a scientific attitude and researches which, when carried out according to scientific laws, could end in contradicting the underlying philosophical principles which prompted the search, and which would therefore have to be discarded.

Philosophy is necessary to science in order to save it from narrowness of vision and from a tendency towards self-contemplation. The philosopher, like the poet, takes an overall view of things. He looks at the forest as well as the trees, and he surveys the landscape with an all-embracing gaze, from a distance; therefore, although he may miss details, he may also, like an observer in an aeroplane, discover geographical structures and traces of ancient constructions which could not be detected by anyone simply walking over the same ground. Like the poet, the philosopher is not so much concerned with the phenomenal appearance of the various aspects of being as with the vision of his inner eye, that is to say with his imagination which can descry, beyond appearances, the images of the true reality which is part of the wholeness of essence. The difference between the philosopher and the poet is that the philosopher's system must hold together and be able to stand the criticism of both speculative and practical reason, and that though it may have flaws, illogicalities or errors of detail, it must have a general logical wholeness. Poets or artists do not have a system, or, if like Dante they have one, it is a borrowed one and it is used to serve the poet's or artist's ends. What counts in this case is the coherence, beauty and truth of the work of art as a whole, and its truth is not measured by verifiable, logical criteria, but by criteria which relate it to the truth and perenniality of being.

A work of art is true in as far as it expresses the true reality of being at a given moment of time, and also beyond that moment, for the whole of Time. As Aristotle put it: 'Poetry is something more philosophical and more true than history, because it deals with universals, while history only deals with particulars, and because the apprehension of the universal or of the intelligible takes place without any use of language as discourse, and without abstractions.' It takes place through concrete, sensuous images and metaphors fused into symbolic entities which reveal the profound, inter-subjective truth of a given age, which is also a universal truth. Such revelations, analogous to mystical revelations, are carried out without any conceptualization, and through purely sensuous means which are mediated by imagination at the level of essences. This does not mean that art is either divagation or merely wayward inspiration, moving at random, without rational control, orientation or finality. On the contrary, art is essentially rational, but the rationality by which it is guided is not conceptual, analytical rationality, but the true rationality of Being, operating at the level of pure intuition or will-to-existence, which precedes and informs creation, while on the contrary conceptual reason can only emanate from creation.

Creative reason or will-to-existence makes itself known through the mysterious laws of genius which mediates true essence into existence, and therefore expresses the hidden will or eternal principle of being. The music of Mozart, Rembrandt's paintings, the creation of Lear—in Baudelaire's words, 'everything that is beautiful and noble is the result of reason and reflection.' The reason here involved is, of course, imagination, the faculty which grasps unseen analogies and contrasts, and restores them to oneness. It is the faculty through which the forms or essential principles which cause the completion and the perfection of all things reveal through existence their true ontological secret.

The philosopher and the artist accept the fact that light necessarily entails darkness, and that being carries with it an unsolvable margin of mystery. Science, which deals with separate aspects of being, believes that the complete truth of the aspects which it seeks to explore can be reached, and by so doing it ignores the important role played by nothingness in the unfolding of being. The pursuit of science is objective, while the pursuit of philosophy has been, until it was recently reduced, in certain cases, to a parody or a servant of science, metaphysical, that is to say always dealing with being in general as well as with its relationship to Being, and also, of course, the existence of the thinking being. This pursuit and its searches, if they are honest, are a matter of life and death.

Scientific truth is its own finality and it leaves the question of life and death to the philosopher or, in some cases, to the state. Another problem is that if the scientist attempts to extrapolate from the truth obtained from a fragment of being to the whole of being, he can only produce a laboratory-made Frankensteinian robot, whose only humanity lies in the hands of the scientist who manipulates it. The philosopher, whether he is Plato or Kant, knows through his knowledge that he will never know the essential, true reality or noumenal world. He knows that there are things which he will never know. The scientist, on the other hand, knows that in the field of knowledge in which he is operating there are no limits. The philosopher generally begins his work on a level which he knows will not divulge the final answer, and he tries to expound his search in logical systems in which all the aspects of being can be understood. The scientist moves only in a chosen domain of investigation in which pragmatic, verifiable results can be obtained. The philosopher is, on the whole, concerned with what being could be or might be, and nowadays he can only attempt such a task if he has a reasonable knowledge of the basic principles of science, and this is something which has become more and more difficult, if not impossible. This difficulty might help to explain the growing impossibility of metaphysics.

This state of affairs seems to leave greater and greater scope to science, and this in turn leads certain apologists of science, who wrongly equate culture with knowledge, to propound the notion that culture should be unified instead of being divided, as it is now supposed to be, into scientific and humanistic strands. According to this view, it seems that culture could be unified if the élite, the educated, were as proficient in science as they are in the humanities and the arts, and vice versa. Leaving aside the vital point that there is absolutely no ground for reducing the meaning of the word 'culture' to a question of education and knowledge, thus ignoring its normal anthropological meaning which basically expresses a given, complex and complete way of life, it is evident that nowadays it is less possible than ever to be equally proficient in science and the humanities. In fact, equal proficiency in art and science has never been possible. If some modern scientists possess, to different extents, a limited knowledge of philosophy or of the arts, it is most unlikely that a poet or a painter could be seriously conversant with the intricacies and the complexities of the latest scientific discoveries in physics, astronomy or medicine. Even Valéry, who was remarkably well-equipped for mathematics and for scientific thinking, was never more than an amateur in these domains, and no doubt had he been a better scientist, he would have been a far lesser poet. Aeschylus and Phidias were certainly unlikely to have been able to follow the calculations of Thales or of Pythagoras. Racine could no more have grasped the mathematics of Pascal than Shakespeare could have grasped those of Copernicus. Even the unique Leonardo Da Vinci was not a mathematician. This kind of universal proficiency is neither possible nor necessary. The nature of the truths which the scientist and the artist pursue is different, though philosophically related and destined to affect, in various degrees, the human mind and the growth of man.

The notion that since the prerequisites for equal proficiency in art and science are not inherently part of human nature, they should be supplied through education and social pressures, so as to produce what is called a unified culture, is unsound and ultimately useless. It is as useless as the notion that culture, in the narrow sense of refinement of taste and manners, is incompatible with violence and cruelty. According to this view, love of the music of Beethoven, Bach and Mozart, or of the paintings of Raphael and Giotto, should immunize those who possess it and preclude in them any displays of inhuman cruelty and criminal behaviour. This is to reduce art to a kind of perfect orchid sprung from and living in a vacuum, and to forget its environment, the manure required to make it grow. It is to think of man as a single-channel television set which, once it has been put together, can receive only one given set of transmissions and give out only one set of reactions. It is demonstrably far from facts.

A man may love Mozart's music and yet be an egoist and, even worse, a cruel sadist. Music is what it is; it teaches neither bad nor good behaviour. It is music; it engenders an experience

which does not necessarily shape our moral compulsion towards the good or the bad, or, least of all, control our instincts
for the good. It all depends on what the human being who
listens to music makes of it. A cacophony might enrage a mad-
man and push him into a fit of violence, but a Mozart sonata
would be no good to a shipwrecked, starving man in the middle
of the ocean, whose desperate needs are reduced to a boat and
bread. Achievements in the arts, or in science, are no guaran-
tees for good morality. The age of Da Vinci and Michelangelo
was also the age of Sforza, Borgia and other *condottieri* whose
violence and lawlessness were neither disturbed nor assuaged
by the majesty of Leonardo's *Last Supper* or by that of the
Rondanini Pietà. Leonardo himself painted the *Last Supper* and
the *Madonna of the Rocks*—and also eagerly helped Ludovic
il More to build engines of war so as to kill as many men as
possible. It is clearly nonsense to believe that because the cour-
tiers of Louis XIV could enjoy Racine's elegant verse and heart-
rending tragedies, or Claude Le Lorrain's and Poussin's paintings,
they should have behaved towards one another like perfect
Franciscan monks. They raped, poisoned and murdered, and
they happily served in the savage Thirty Years' War which
decimated central Europe in the seventeenth century, and they
gladly countenanced and participated in the revocation of the
Edict of Nantes, in the same spirit in which their ancestors had
taken part in the St Bartholomew massacre a hundred years
before.

Culture, in the restricted sense in which the word is generally
used, is no guarantee of civilized, moral behaviour. Civilized
behaviour is not a matter of culture, artistic taste or love of
the arts; it is a matter of moral principles, based on the sacredness of the individual. Now it seems to me impossible to confine
ethics to the purely temporal plane, or to confer upon it an
autonomy which excludes transcendence, though I am prepared
to respect the humanist point of view, if it is based on a notion
of man as part of a whole and informed with a sense of purpose,
and if it grants equal value and importance to all the compon-

ent elements of man's make-up. The word 'God' may now be objectionable to many, confusing to some, and simply meaningless to many others. But His predicate—Being—which implies the perenniality of spirit or essence, and of absolute goodness, can be accepted and recognized as the basis of life. If these prerequisites are accepted, they can provide a truly human basis for life. The Greeks of the age of Pericles were undeniably great, in more than one respect—philosophy, poetry, mathematics, tragedy, even war—but they did not set store by individual human life. Men were born to die, cruelly or in their beds. The way to the end did not matter, and not even their numerous demi-gods could escape untimely death. In fact, even the gods were threatened by it and were subject to the will of the Fates. It took Socrates and Plato to outline the notion of the immortality and the anxiety of the individual soul in the face of the eternal, whose necessary purification for salvation prefigures Christianity.

In spite of their marvellous political system, the Greeks of the great age of Athens were profoundly inhuman. The slaves, and they were numerous, mattered less than beasts. Yet, amidst this inhumanity, they happened to produce, all in all, probably the most extraordinary blossoming of genius that the world has ever known. The conclusion of this argument is that genius does not exclude inhumanity of behaviour, any more than inhumanity could be said to be a prerequisite for the flowering of genius. These supposed relationships of causes and effects are the result of the kind of pseudo-scientific observations which some Lysenko of history or of philosophy might indulge in, but which no reputable philosopher or historian could for a moment accept. The world is full of complexities. The strangest plants, the strangest aspects of life, can flourish side by side as parts of the general versatility and changeability of man, who can be both, at the same time or in turns, angel and demon, good and bad, open to spiritual experiences—artistic or otherwise—or cesspools of desires. 'Culture' will not make man into a humane, compassionate, tolerant human being.

The deaths in Vietnam, Bengal, Auschwitz, by napalm bomb, starvation or gas chambers, were instigated neither by culture nor by science. Only a certain attitude to man and to life could put an end to such cruelties, and this attitude would have to be pervaded with the notion of spirit, which is transcendent, and with that of human brotherhood. For the moment these two notions are anything but widely accepted, but neither are they completely absent from the life of mankind. The murderous war in Vietnam provoked strong revulsions, questionings and protests even in the United States. The atrocities committed by West Pakistan in Bengal prompted India, already plagued by poverty and starvation, to take up the task of feeding and housing millions of refugees. The holocaust of the Jews in the last World War has seared the human conscience and will never be erased from the human mind, which has understood that these hounded people must have a shelter of their own against persecutions.

The spirit of man can flicker like embers in the wind, but it cannot be put out. This is cause for confidence in the future, for whatever its ups and downs, mankind must needs reach its end which is spirit.

8

Science and Wisdom

In the previous chapter I attempted to outline the differences between philosophy and science, and the need to integrate science into a body of religious or ethical values which could give life coherence and purpose. A society which reduces human values to experiment and verification, and fails to realize that values are essentially spiritual and never intrinsically epistemological or purely historical, is bound to end in some kind of Orwellian society in which a handful of scientists and technocrats, acting as Big Brothers, watch, through closed-circuit television, the behaviour of their dehumanized, Frankensteinian slaves and amorphous fellow-beings, who work, eat, drink, sleep or copulate mechanically and mindlessly, unaware of, or unconcerned by, any notion of past or future, and living only in the present. Epistemology can no more be the foundation of morality or of the meaning and purpose of life than scientific, sociological, biological or anthropological truths can provide such meaning or purpose.

Life is a whole, including nature, and man is part of it, and therefore subject to its laws. As Voltaire put it: 'It would be very singular that all nature, all the planets should obey eternal laws, and that there should be a little animal, five feet high, who, in contempt of these laws, could act as he pleased, solely according to his caprice.' Two centuries later, in the 1953 Reith Lectures, J. R. Oppenheimer said: 'For most of us, in most of those moments when we were most free of corruption, it has been the beauty of the world of nature and the strange and compelling harmony of its order that has sustained, inspired and led us.' In ancient and in modern times, men in the higher reaches of science, Heraclitus, Kepler, Pascal, Whitehead or Einstein, understand the harmony of nature and the multipicity of the roads which lead to truth. They do not confine truth to experiment and the verifiability of hypotheses and concepts; they know that the truth of religion or of art cannot be verified by scientific measurements, and they know also that this truth is as valid as scientific truths, and as necessary to human life. They know that objective facts and the notion of pure objectivity are a myth, and that the laws of nature are discovered and organized by man, therefore that they are not lying ready-made in the dark waiting to be revealed or reproduced, as a photographer reproduces the likeness of a person or of a landscape. They know that philosophers, artists and scientists are not recording machines, but human beings endowed with mental and affective structures, the combinations of inborn traits and acquired knowledge. Therefore they always look at life and nature through these ideas, categories or hypotheses which they seek to verify through scientific tests or to transform into symbolic entities through words, colours, volumes, lines of musical notes. The philosopher, the artist or the scientist always seeks to impose upon his material the rigour, precision and coherence which translate into understandable or apprehensible terms what his intuition has suggested to his heart or to his mind, or both. A creative genius always imposes, in varying degrees, his mark, in science, philosophy or the arts, or on whatever type of experience he seeks to illuminate. Einstein made this point in 1918: 'Man tries to form a simplified and clear conception of the world in a manner somehow adequate to himself, and to conquer the world of reality by replacing it to a certain extent by this picture. The painter, the poet, the speculative philosopher, and the naturalist do it, each of them, in his own way. He places in this picture the centre of gravity of his emotional life in order to find the tranquillity and constancy which he cannot find within the narrow limits of turbulent personal experience.'

Limited rationalism, that is to say practical reason dissociated from the original Greek rationalism which included speculative reason and both mystical and mythical experience, broke the oneness of human experience, separated immanence from transcendence, practical from speculative reason, and after scepticism, encyclopaedism, materialism and a positivism obsessed with light and progress, finally ended in anthropomorphic nihilism. Rousseau's mystical belief in nature was replaced by faith in culture, something which was later taken over by Marx. His mythical faith in the righteousness of the will of the people was swept aside by the rise of the myth of money and power, which trampled down the people or led them by the nose through the skilful manipulation of their longings and their misery. Kant's belief in speculative reason as a basis of metaphysics, Schopenhauer's transcendence of the will, and Hegel's rationalistic idealism and belief in the completion and perfection of Being through becoming, close the circle of metaphysical thinking begun with the Greeks, and mark a new beginning, or cycle, which starts from chaos, or from the nothingness of annihilated values.

This nihilistic phase of European history coincided with the collapse of the French Revolution which combined Rousseau's messianism with eighteenth-century rationalism, with the end of the Napoleonic dream of establishing a universal order, and with the rise and growth of industrialism in Europe and in the USA. The dawn of the French Revolution and of the French Empire, hailed with enthusiasm by all the great Romantic poets of the age, moved through a brief high noon into darkness. The individual genius, the Hegelian incarnation of the *Zeitgeist* working to bring about the dominance of universal spirit, the agent for the operation which Shelley described in the words: 'the everlasting universe of things flows through the mind', was steadily swept aside by the growth of bourgeois mediocrity and materialism. What remained of the belief that history was led by Providence towards an inscrutable yet beneficent end, or by an informing, Hegelian world spirit

working towards greater and greater consciousness and perfection, dwindled into mock religiosity represented by spiritualism, materialism and worship of science and knowledge as
means of salvation, and revolutionary nihilism. These four
aspects of human thought, which represent the main latent
forces of the society of the second half of the nineteenth
century, underline one single, fundamental weakness, which is
the absence of a unifying belief—religious or mythical—which
could hold society together.

Both religion and myth imply ethics and aesthetics; the
Greek myths are both ethical and aesthetic, and Judaic mono-
theism is also not only ethical and history-minded, but aesthetic
too. The 'Song of Songs', the great stories of the Bible, have the
coherence and transcendental illumination of works of art in
their own right, irrespective of the religious wisdom which
they convey. In fact, religion must carry with it certain
mythical and mysterious elements which rise to the heroic,
which attracts proselytes, martyrs and men prepared to follow
its teaching because it is ennobling and takes them out of themselves.

The moment religion secularizes itself, as it did from the
seventeenth century onwards, and finds itself most of the time,
at least as far as its hierarchy is concerned, on the side of
established authority, material well-being and short-sighted
conservatism, it is bound to incur the dissaffection and alienation of the poor. If, together with this incapacity to remain
faithful to its roots as a revolutionary, heroic creed,* religion is
also submitted to the demythologizing and demystifying power
of science which seeks to replace it with the myth of scientific
knowledge, then it is bound to fight a losing battle, particularly
if it is also attacked from the inside by members of its own
corpus who question its dogma, challenge its structure and
seek to dispel its mythical elements.

The attitude which consists in trying to appease a fierce

---

* In a famous short note dated 3 May 1926, Bergson wrote: 'Christianity
equals dissatisfaction, *ergo* turning things upside down, *ergo* action.'

opponent by sacrificing to him parts of one's own strength, with the hope of placating him, is never effective. The process of sacrifice and abandonment of positions is bound to follow an ever-accelerated progression, until nothing of oneself is left. The Church does not need to look upon science as a rival, and with few exceptions science does not need to look upon religion as its enemy. Neither attitude is supported by facts. To start from the premise that as long as the Church's authority over society prevailed, science could only thrive by opposing this authority, is to ignore the fact that the founders of the scientific spirit and of experimentalism were, from Erigena to William of Ockham and Roger Bacon, churchmen, that the academies of science in France and in England were in their early days composed largely of devout churchmen, that the British Association for the Advancement of Science was founded on the proposal of a churchman, and that two out of its first three presidents were churchmen. There is no ground for believing that a practising or non-practising Christian cannot be a truly objective-minded scientist. As a member of a God-created world, he necessarily believes that the objective search for the discovery of the laws of nature is part of man's rationality and purpose in life. The fact that Newton was a Christian did not prevent him from discovering the laws of gravitation, any more than his faith prevented Leibnitz from sharing with Newton the discovery of differential calculus. Kepler was no more hampered in his scientific discoveries, which he saw as a homage to God, than Fra Lippo Lippi was prevented from painting good paintings because he was a good Christian. True, there was Galileo, but that was only one of the temporary aberrations of the Church. Locke, Pascal and Newman, all admirable Christians, carefully separated understanding from assent, experimental knowledge from faith. The number of scientists who are also good Christians is legion, and atheism cannot be a prerequisite of science. A Christian, whether he is a scientist, a poet or a painter, does his research or his creative work, not according to religious dogma but according to the principles and the laws of his discipline. These laws and principles are summed up in one major one, which is the objective, untrammelled search for the truth, the only principle by which a man, whether Christian or un-Christian, can keep a pure conscience worthy of God's grace, if he believes in it, as well as of the respect of his fellow-beings.

To know, to classify, to predict certain physical events, to categorize them or to probe the laws which govern the workings of nature or of the human body, is one thing. To equate faith or morality with experimental knowledge is quite another. Technology can and does greatly improve life, but it can also endanger or destroy it, unless it is dominated by the kind of faith in life and the value of the human spirit which controls its application for the good of man. This faith and these values cannot be created or ascertained by scientific means, and though the scientist as a man ought to play a vital part in their application, they are not co-equal with scientific values. Of course the intellectual integrity, the respect for experimental truth, the attempt at objectivity and the concern for the uses to which science is put, are in themselves ingredients of ethics. But the problem is that scientific truth cannot be a basis for morality, which can only rest on religious principles, or on para-religious, humanistic, categorical imperatives, which must posit, if not transcendence, at least the belief in the absolute brotherhood of man and in the sacredness of human life. These religious or para-religious principles form the basis of human experience. They are the deeply felt human longings and beliefs which have moulded the behaviour of men since men passed from the stage of anthropoids to that of men, and though they may not be verifiable by instruments or biological analysis, they are as much part of the human being as the DNA which controls the unfolding and the growth of his cells.

Faith, whether it is the Nietzschean and Schopenhauerian will to power, the Bergsonian *élan vital*, the Hegelian *Zeitgeist*, the Platonic will-to-appearance of Being, or the faith in God of St Augustine and Pascal, is neither a refuge for the weak nor a sign of weakness. The saints, the martyrs, the Jews who in their millions died for their faith, could not be described as weak. The simplistic argument that they died in order to make sure of the Heaven in which they believed can only be the argument of those who know nothing about faith. The essence of faith is not certainty, but uncertainty and anxiety. No man of faith is ever sure of being truly in a state of grace or in perfect accord with the Being of his faith. Consequently he never knows, not even at the point of death, if death will bring to him the kind of eternity he longs for. To claim that faith is the refuge of the weak-minded is to ignore the existence of Einstein, Whitehead, Bergson, Laplace, Kepler and other geniuses.

Facts and faith are not mutually exclusive, but one must not be confused with the other, or judged by the other. Faith is not a physical fact, but an experience which may, and does at times, controvert facts and phenomenal reality. Belief in the spirit is of the same nature. When in 1940 the logical, facts-minded leader of the French forces looked at facts and decreed that France was defeated, De Gaulle ignored facts and said that France would only be defeated if she acknowledged defeat, and if her spirit was totally broken down by facts. Churchill did the same. The facts were against him; he ignored them, put his faith in the courage of his people, and said 'No', confident that as long as a handful of them survived the holocaust, Britain would live. Faith or belief in spiritual values is at times a total denial of facts. Such a denial is only possible in dramatic moments when one has to decide between life and death. That is why the Church, the principal custodian of a given faith, ever dealing with life and death, should know that it can only survive and be a living force, not by trying to come to terms with the scientism, the materialism and the promiscuousness of the age, but by the uncompromising defence of those who formed Christ's audience when He spoke on His Galilean mount. That is to say the humble, the poor, the disinherited—black, yellow or white—the classless and the exploited (whether by ruthless Eastern party bosses or by the demagogues who bamboozle them with promises and dreams of technological Edens).

The limitation of this dream society of technological achievement, instantaneous hedonism and egotistical satisfaction is that its pseudo-rationalism, its orientation towards superficial knowledge and gadgetry, which are the products of vulgarized science, lead only to self-worship. Speculative reason, as defined by Kant, and even the universal reason of the master of positivism, Auguste Comte, who like Kant posited a belief in absolute reason and therefore willynilly in metaphysics, have now been swept aside by the overwhelming tide of nihilism which accompanied the growth of science and which has done away with practically all the dominant values of Western civilization, with the exception of its materialistic aspects. God has been declared dead, and the whole aspect of ethics connected with His existence has been thrown into question. The growth of science, the main corollary of which was the diminution of religion and of metaphysical thinking, underlined at the same time the growing importance of the concept of the irrational, more and more explored by psychologists, from Nietzsche to William James, Freud and Bergson, the growth of spiritualism and, above all, the growth of subjectivism. This subjectivism, whether it expresses itself through the Kierkegaardian assertion that truth is subjective, or the Schopenhauerian and Nietzschean will-to-power as the essence of being, is the natural outcome of the nihilism which followed the clash between science or rather scientism and religion, between positivism and idealism. In this clash, none of the contenders was either truly annihilated or truly victorious, but the final result was a general fragmentation of beliefs and attitudes, out of which religious, political, philosophical, scientific and artistic leaders sought to pick out and to adopt whatever would most conform to their affinities and needs, and to make of these the basis of their work or research.

What was soon most apparent was that there was no longer a centre around which the normally centrifugal forces of society could gravitate. Society had become kaleidoscopic, the bulk of its component elements opting quite naturally for scientism and for the materialism which brought them wealth and well-being, while they looked upon art as adornment for their lives and homes, or as a kind of escape into a dream world, and upon religion as a kind of Pontius Pilate's weekly washing of hands which enabled them to continue to gather their weekly profits with calm consciences and cleansed souls. Artists and thinkers whose imagination could not so easily be drugged or satisfied by such palliatives could not but repudiate a reality which was merely shadow without substance, and adopt on the whole a nihilistic and subjective attitude to life. Freed from academism and from the desire to please the broad public, they were intent above all on facing up to the truth as they felt it and thought it, and on bringing it to light, whatever the cost. They were aware of the collapse of established values, therefore they were nihilistic; they were aware of the shortcomings of reason and of language as means of conveying the whole human experience, and of the impossibility of examining objectively phenomenal reality and of finding the truth in it. The only approach to truth was therefore tentative, subjective and aimed at essences and not appearances. The appearances were left to science and to naturalism, from Courbet to Zola. The dominant aspects of art—Symbolism and Cubism—were less direct, more allusive, more laden with references and more transcendental. They moved away from eighteenth-century sensitivity and sentimentality, and from Romantic sensuousness, to a blend of intellect and the senses, as may be seen, irrespective of their religious or non-religious beliefs, in the poetry of Baudelaire, Valéry, Claudel, Yeats, Rilke or Eliot; or to highly intellectualized, subjective creations, as may be seen in the work of Mallarmé, Cubism or Constructionism. The truth, for a poet like Mallarmé, is the poem itself—a symbolic entity embodying a creative, heuristic instant during which the poet and the truth which he reveals are a transcendental flight from nowhere to nowhere. They are examples of being reduced to will-in-action, that is to say, they are examples of perfect nihilism.

Nihilism, the attitude of mind or philosophy best expressed by Nietzsche, embracing Kierkegaard as well as Kafka and, up to a point, Valéry, Sartre, Anouilh and others, can be said to be one of the main elements of art and philosophy of the last eighty years or so. It is a form of subjective idealism, which, although it does not dominate them, does not leave unaffected philosophers as diverse as Bradley, Bergson and Heidegger, to say nothing of Sartre. The latter two, particularly Sartre, are described as existentialists, therefore in principle remote from idealism, yet their subjectivism, and above all their concept of nothingness, which for Sartre is the basis of creativity and freedom, is an idealistic concept.

Nihilism is by its very nature extremely difficult to define. Like mystical experience, to which it is methodologically related and to which it can lead, it can only be apprehended negatively. The error to avoid is that of looking upon it as a positive entity to be credited with positive attributes. Yet, though it is not a positive ens, it is not only part of Being, it can also be equated negatively with Being, for if Being did not also contain non-Being, there would be no possibility of the existence of becoming as the creativity of Being. Consequently Being would be absolute, immutable and perfect, that is to say absolute nothingness. This would be a contradiction in terms, therefore Being must carry the concept of non-Being as the negation of Being. The two notions are inseparable yet not identical, in the sense that total identity or oneness is prevented by becoming, which is the being of Being, and as such Becoming can have neither beginning nor end; it is; and therefore, like Being, it has always been and it will always be.

Nihilism is the concept of the absence, or rather of the negation, of Being, the necessity of which has not escaped the most fervent atheist, such as Nietzsche or Sartre. It is a way of knowing one aspect of Being, which is in a state of obfuscation or eclipse, but not a denial of the concept of Being, without which the concept of non-Being is not conceivable. The word 'nihilism' is generally used not in Nietzschean terms of will-to-power and transmutation of values, but merely in order to indicate an attitude of mind implying, in varying degrees, the negation of the values which for eighteen centuries have dominated Western life. This attitude has been described as irrational, and in our science-minded age the word 'irrational' is liberally used by those who wish to denigrate or to dismiss anyone who does not share the dogmatic belief in the power of reason, which for them means practical reason. Thus, Bergson, Bradley, Teilhard de Chardin, each asserting in his own way the transcendence and immanence of Being, intent upon becoming and perfectibility, are dismissed as irrational. Yet this type of so-called irrationalism, condemned in the name of practical reason, is nothing less, in fact, than Kant's speculative reason, or the *nous* of Plato, capable of embracing the life of the ideas and the imagination, the intelligible life of the mind as well as the life of practical reason.

The cleavage between speculative and practical reason, which brought about the partial eclipse of metaphysics, and that of humanistic rationalism which looked upon the world and phenomenal reality as apprehensible to reason, has fostered the growth of scientism, which aims at submitting all aspects of life—religious, political and ethical—to science and to the intellect, and that of an anti-intellectual, anti-rational attitude to life. So we have scientific Marxism, scientific linguistics, scientific history, psychology, etc.—but none of these disciplines can be called truly scientific. The claims of Marxism to be the scientific doctrine which will correct the ills of society and bring about the millennium are repudiated by those who find its determinism irreconcilable with the freedom and objectivity of research, while the political finality which in the communist countries insists upon submitting all aspects of life to control by the state is unacceptable to any truly rational being.

The anti-intellectual attitude in fact comprises various aspects of opposition to scientism, which it would be wrong to lump together under one single category. The Freudian belief in the importance of the subconscious, the belief of Bergson in the *élan vital* or that of Gabriel Marcel in the subjectivity of truth, are not examples of irrationalism, but assertions of the continuous interpenetration of transcendence and immanence. This so-called irrationalism is very different from the irrationalism of the expressionists, the surrealists, the action painters, the drop-outs, the hippies, the primitivists, and the searchers for unreal or illuminating experiences and oblivion through drugs. All these people find the world irrational, and its endless wars and its mass murders and brutalities totally alien to any truly humane values. Therefore, whether their names be Rimbaud, Gauguin, Utrillo, Van Gogh or Mayakovsky, they opt out of society through exile, madness or suicide. The world of their art is the world of their hearts and minds, and not the world of the unbearable phenomenal reality in which they live.

The Western world, a world apparently devoted to rationalism, which began to fall apart from the moment when reason became purely anthropomorphic, and ceased being a link between phenomenal reality and the Idea or Being informing it, has produced the most violent outbursts of irrationalism that mankind has ever known: Nazism, Fascism, the slaughter of the Jews, the terrors and the bloodbaths of Stalinism, and the savage wars supposedly meant to contain communism which make a mockery of progress and pretences of civilization. Art has sought refuge in pure sensualism, subjectivism, Negro primitivism, pop art, collages, happenings, gimmicky pieces of engineering giving the masses the illusion that they are participating in and enjoying art, or in ever more abstruse intellectualizations and conceptualizations. The trend towards intellectualization is so strong that in France, for instance, there are critics who dare to say that the writer does not understand his work until it has been conceptualized by the critic, and those who assert that the commentary that they write about a work is equivalent to the work of art itself. One cannot go further towards the worship of ratiocination and the denigration of the imagination, which implies at its best the capacity to incarnate the ideas apprehended by and intelligible to speculative reason.

Religion and myth, religious or political, are at a low ebb. Only the myth of nationhood survives, and is in fact gaining strength in the name of the principle of self-determination. While a sense of national identity and shared traditions is and could be a means of resisting the conformism and the pressures of big blocks intent upon spreading their power, a sense of human brotherhood is certainly of greater importance and value. The truth is that although politicians try, for their own political reasons, to exalt the feelings of nationhood, these feelings are overridden in the West by the capitalist forces which control production, employment and the electoral system, and in the East, with few exceptions, by the military forces of the ideology and the party in power which ride roughshod over private sensibilities or indeed anything which stands in the path of the preservation of their power.

The proletariat of the Western world has ceased to exist as a class because it has ceased to have a class consciousness. The proletariat now only exists in the form of the blacks in the USA, and the disinherited populations of South America and the underdeveloped countries of Africa and Asia, which are the true proletariat of the Western world, knocking at its door and asking for a better share of the advantages of modern technology and redress for the injustices of the past. Whether in the Western world or in the Soviet Union or China, the authority of the state is increasing. In the communist countries people feel more and more helpless and do not, on the whole, try to protest, and in the West people are worried by their incapacity to influence the decisions of the state and its administration. Therefore they feel disaffected, alienated, and not an integral part of the national entity to which they are supposed to belong. This feeling militates strongly against the strength of the national feelings which the state seeks to maintain by devious means, the most commonly used being the threat of foreign intervention or aggression.

The alienation of the underdeveloped countries, the revolt of the blacks, the disaffection of the young and their partial withdrawal from Western society, are telling signs of the acuteness of the disease which they cannot cure, because power is not in their hands, and because those who wield it will, if necessary, use it in order to crush them. Yet their protest is important, for it is the only way to force upon the consciousness of those in authority the awareness that changes are required and that, if these changes are not brought about, the disease will eventually infect even countries like the Soviet Union where the state and its military machine rule absolutely. There must be a change of heart; this change must take place in the mind also, and it must consist in a shift from limited, practical reason and scientism to the wholeness of reason which includes darkness and light, the intelligible as well as the experimentally verifiable world, the spiritual as well as the material elements of life, the advantages of technology as well as the greater advantages of freedom and human dignity—two fundamental concepts which, according to a leading American behaviourist, are now declared outdated and should, according to him, be replaced by the woolly notion of behavioural science.

In order to heal the divisions between men, man must begin by healing the division within himself. This division affects the vast numbers of men who have discarded the sense and the awareness of transcendence, that is to say, the sense of the wholeness and perenniality of life, and have put their faith in science and science alone, as the only all-embracing basis of a better life. That the word 'science' is synonymous with progress is as undeniable as the fact that this progress is most welcome to mankind. But the vital problem, the problem which modern man must solve or perish as the victim of his own uncontrolled, dehumanized mental agility, is the problem of distinguishing between the possibilities and virtues of science, and the fantasies which are attributed to it in all aspects of life. This problem consists in distinguishing between the truly great scientists who are generally great mathematicians endowed with the imagination of great philosophers and poets, and the lower ranges of science which include the technocrats who, because they lack imagination, display a dogmatism and an intransigent love of scientific method which they exhibit as a badge of superiority over those who are not scientists or science-minded, and which they wish to apply to all aspects of life.

Great philosophers like Husserl or Heidegger, or great scientists like Einstein, accept the fact that now it is well-nigh impossible to be both a great scientist and a great philosopher. Philosophy and science, that is to say modern science, are condemned to be separated, and though it is possible to think of a philosophy of science, it is not possible to think of a scientific or a science-governed philosophy. One can say that up to Hegel, who was the last founder of a coherent philosophical system, philosophy was on the whole the rational knowledge of the phenomenal and noumenal world as well as of the various methods used in order to know reality in all its aspects. After Hegel knowledge became fragmented, and there was no longer any connection between positivistic, experimental knowledge and metaphysical knowledge. Philosophy turned towards psychological and existential aspects of knowledge, towards phenomenalism and questions of meaning with Husserl, and existential hermeneutics with Heidegger.

The scientist can reflect on science or on the aspects of science in which he works, and he can up to a point relate these aspects to wider concepts, but unless he is a philosopher, he is reduced to using concepts which he has neither tested nor submitted to any serious critique. Above all, he is not in control of the various meanings of these concepts as they are applied in the various philosophical systems. Therefore, any attempt by scientists to deal with philosophical problems involves certain philosophical prerequisites which are more or less coincidental with the notion of what a philosophy of science could be. These prerequisites, reduced to the minimum, imply the capacity to explain logically the structure and the coherence of the theories discussed, and a reasonable knowledge of the genesis of the concepts used, together with their various historical connotations. Finally they imply an awareness of the dividing line between the two disciplines and of the problems which have not yet been conceptualized or cannot be conceptualized, and therefore must be discarded as unmanageable in the present state of knowledge. Any critical examination of a philosophical system or ideology can only be done systematically, logically, through the use of concepts already defined, and above all by always relating the aspect examined to the coherence to which it belongs. To discuss the deterministic aspect of Marxism in isolation from the basic economic and psychological structure of Marx's analysis of Western society at a given time, or to isolate what one calls the idealism of Hegel from the coherence of his wide-ranging philosophical system, and to retain from it only what could be called its non-existential, non-individualistic aspect, is not to apply critical, objective criteria to philosophy, but to use certain aspects of a philosophical system to shore up an argument.

Leibnitz's dream of turning speech into an algebra of the mind, and truth into mathematical equation, has been a dream that all great mathematicians from Pythagoras to Einstein have pursued but which they have known to be inapplicable to the whole of life as an historico-social phenomenon. They know that life can be inspired and guided by numbers, by pure mathematics which expresses the higher laws and the ideas which are at the heart of the moving permanence of the universe, but they also know that thought, at the philosophical, religious, ethical and artistic levels, can neither be turned into algebra nor formalized. They do not dream of reducing ethics to scientific laws, and art or philosophy to scientific experiment. They know that these various activities are part of the whole man whose sensuousness and spirituality cannot be reduced to those of a perfectly controlled, robot-like animal. They leave these ambitions to lesser scientists, and to the fellow-travellers of science in the arts, in philosophy, linguistics, politics and technology, who are convinced that they can enhance their work and confer profundity upon it by wrapping it up in scientific terminology or by stretching it on scientific Procrustean beds which are totally incompatible with these disciplines, which cannot be equated with science.

The great cleavage and conflict is between man as a worshipper of science as the only thing that matters on earth, and man as a believer that religion, philosophy, art and humanism, though not assessable by science, are yet a vital part of the essence of man's rationality into which science must be integrated so that its fruits truly benefit the humanization of humanity. Without this integration, science, not fully informed with and controlled by morality, is exploited by power-seekers who use it as it suits them, and all too often for war and for the destruction of mankind. However honest, well-meaning, altruistic and humane true scientists may be, they are only a small part of a society ruled by politicians who are corruptible because of their lust for power and who always seek to secure the scientists' support for the fulfilment of their plans which, consciously or unconsciously, are more often than not entangled in self-interest. Scientists can be lured or deluded by all sorts of apparently honourable motives, such as promises of money for research, patriotism, honours, national prestige, etc., and unless they enter fully into the life of the community and accept a code of ethics based not on science—for that is an illusion—but on the belief in the sacredness of human life, and unless they use all their collective efforts all over the world in order to defend this principle, mankind will go on living on the verge of disaster. 'The greatest problem for man', said Kant, 'is to know what man must do in order to be man.' This problem consists in establishing just and true foundations for moral thought and behaviour, and this can only be done by listening to the true voice, or categorical imperative, of conscience, which is the voice of practical as well as of metaphysical reason.   Beyond the Nietzschean assertion of the death of God, an assertion which is meaningless, and which possesses only metaphorical value as a basis for the renewal of outmoded ethics, the most important problem of our age, which is the age of science, is the problem which can be stated in Kantian terms of the gap between practical and speculative reason, that is to say between phenomenalist, positivist or empirical reason, and speculative reason which even in our times still affords the possibility of purely mathematical or abstract metaphysics. Whether God is dead or alive cannot be settled by science, though linguistic positivism can at least prove that the phrase 'God is dead' is meaningless, for the word 'God' cannot be used with a predicate which negates the essence of the subject. But this is not the point; the point is that the split in human reason, and the reduction of the role of human reason to experimental observation, description and a repertory of facts, has led to the self-worship of reason, and the philosophy of science which emanates from it to pure and simple subjective materialism.

Whatever the upholders of this philosophic attitude may say, whether they be Mach, Besso or the modern biologists, their phenomenalistic positivism, rooted in Bacon, Hobbes, and partly in Locke, claims a kind of Cartesian division of subject from object as the foundation of their objectivity, ignoring of course Descartes' metaphysics, and insists on the pre-eminence of the experience of the senses as the only basis for epistemology, which thus becomes, according to them, a basis for ethics. This boils down to utilitarianism, behaviourism, observation and recording of facts, which become the source of pyramidal deductions towards theories and systems and extrapolations which easily impress the believers in this limited rationalism.

Positivism—scientific or linguistic—is only valuable for cleansing, pruning or opening up thickly wooded areas, but has little or nothing to contribute to creativeness in any field of human thought. Its basic materialism excludes both the notion and the existence of the wholeness of the universe, of which man is an integral part, and therefore subjectively imprinted with its laws and inner structures which, at the level of genius, he can recognize or reveal. This is the world of ancient and modern mathematicians, from the Greeks to Leibnitz, Einstein or Planck. It is a world which the latter two describe in not very dissimilar terms.

In an essay published in 1931 Planck wrote: 'Until very recently no-one questioned the principle of causality; now even this principle has been thrown overboard . . . As a physicist I feel entitled to put forward some of my views about the present situation in physics. Positivistic theory essentially maintains that there is no other source of knowledge except the direct and brief road of perceptions through the senses. Positivism has always rigorously abided by this law. Yet the two propositions: (a) there is a real external world which exists independently from our act of knowing it, and (b) the real external world is not directly knowable, form together the cornerstone upon which rests the whole structure of physics. And yet there is a certain contradiction between these two propositions, and this betrays the presence of an irrational or mystical element which sticks to physics as to any other branch of human knowledge. That's why science is never in a position to give a complete and exhaustive solution of the problems which it confronts.'[1] This conclusion is the kernel of the present study, the main plea of which is for the acceptance of the existence of a certain fringe of mystery, and for the rejection of the nefarious belief in the infinite potentialities of limited reason.

Einstein wrote an unpublished introduction to this article of Planck's in which he said: 'May I be allowed to say that the way in which Planck conceives the present logical situation as well as his subjective expectations about the future evolution of our science entirely correspond to what I also think.' Einstein believed in the objective reality of the universe and in the power of the imagination or speculative reason to intuitively apprehend aspects of its truth. This present study began with a quotation from Einstein, and nothing could express more concisely my thoughts and beliefs than the words which he addressed to Max Born in 1944:[2] 'What you and I expect from science places us now at opposite poles. You believe in a God Who plays dice, and I believe in the perfect rule of the law in a universe in which there is something objective, which I endeavour to grasp in a fiercely speculative manner.' As Max Born put it, he had faith in the powers with which reason is endowed in order to intuit the laws according to which God has constructed the universe.[3]

Referring to the question of scientific method and scientists, Einstein wrote in 1935: 'I advise you to stick closely to one principle; don't listen to their words, fix your attention on their deeds.'[4] The fact is that there is not one single scientific method, but various aspects of the search for truth, and the greatest mistake one could make would certainly be that of reducing them all to the inductive method, based on pure facts. There are no pure facts; they are all coloured by the understanding, the learning and the affectivity of him who records them. There is no search for facts without some hypothesis or theory consciously or subconsciously guiding the search. As Claude Bernard put it: 'To experiment without a preconceived idea is to wander aimlessly.' No search for or observation of facts is ever 'objective'. Notwithstanding his denials, Newton also started from hypotheses or theories without which the fall of an apple in his garden would no more have disturbed his thoughts than the flutter of a feather in the wind.

Facts are not starting points, but the confirmation or refutation of what the mind or imagination has conceived, and to reduce knowledge to induction or to positivistic observations and empiricism is to deprive human reason of its most important and vital part which is the imagination, and to turn men into perfect computers which record linearly and without any interference all the data that are fed into them. The human senses are the servants of the mind, and the mind has many mansions, not all filled with computerized accounts of the life of the earth and the universe. One of them, and not the least important, contains the dreams of its origins, and the light which guides and gives life a purpose, which is no Sisyphian, stoic disdain for absent or hostile gods, but an all-embracing faith in the fraternal and harmonizing powers of unified Reason.

9

Approaches to Knowledge

For in fact, nothing do we know for having seen it; for the truth is hidden in the deep.   DEMOCRITUS

It is not in the nature or character of man to possess true knowledge, though it is in the divine nature . . . He who does not expect the unexpected will not detect it; for him it will remain undetectable and unapproachable.   HERACLITUS

Our civilization started, not with collecting observations, but with bold theories about the world . . . Once we realize that all scientific statements are hypotheses, guesses or conjectures, and that a vast majority of these conjectures (including Bacon's own) have turned out to be false, the Baconian myth becomes irrelevant.
KARL POPPER: *Conjectures and Refutations*

The principle of objectivity, as a concept, is a non-starter; it is an uneasy compound of two words belonging to two different realms. One of these words—'principle'—belongs to the world of *a priori* truths or axioms, unarguable or demonstrably evident and verifiable by experience. The second word—'objectivity'— is a very arguable and fluid philosophical concept which cannot be given an aura of unquestionable truth by being conjoined with a mathematical, pre-conceptual term. One can understand and repeatedly test the principle of Archimedes, but one cannot understand, and even less test, a so-called principle of objectivity. Man is both subject and object, phenomenon and noumenon. As subject, he registers perceptions through the senses, not as a mere camera or mechanical instrument, but as a living organism which consciously or subconsciously organizes perceptions according to the concepts of his understanding which structures what it receives, or through his imagination or pure reason which schematizes or essentializes the real into a form of knowledge which is pre-conceptual. All these mental operations vary according to the affectivity and the essential structures of the understanding and of the imagination of the recording subject.

Imagination, understanding and sensibility form the human mind, and it is the mind which perceives. The senses are nothing more than prehending organs which connect the outside world, the world of phenomena, with the mind, which knows itself through its apprehension of the phenomenal world, or through concepts—whether they are pure concepts or concepts of the understanding. The mind knows itself, not as pure thought—a contradiction in terms—but as a thinking *I*, therefore as self-knowing knowledge.

The mind is not a virgin disc registering the imprint of perceptions; this type of pure phenomenalism is an impossibility, in spite of Husserlian attempts at keeping essential or ontological aspects of consciousness in parenthesis. The mind is a structured organism transforming perceived data as well as intuited representations and schemata of reality into knowledge. This transformation is shaped and controlled by the existing structures of the understanding and the imagination which select what is required in order to fit the categories of the understanding or the pre-schemata or forms of the imagination. The phenomenal world and pure intuitions, some of which are transcendental, like the notions of space and time, are mediated or apprehended according to the essence or form which is the pure, timeless *I*, knowing himself, or revealing being through time. The result of this apprehension, a marriage, a fusion of two essences—that of the apprehended thing or experience and that of the apprehending *I*—can be embodied into images, symbols or organic entities in which sense and thought are fused into the oneness of true knowledge.

The mind contains in varying degrees the ideas or forms of the structures and relationships of the natural world, and knowledge is, in fact, a progressive revelation or discovery of these structures and laws which the mind cognizes directly through the intuition of pure reason, or re-cognizes through perceptions which it assimilates through concepts and words and turns into storable and transmissible knowledge. Both percepts and the understanding of things through concepts are mediated into unified knowledge, through pure intuition or imagination, which is Time individuated and lived as a subject or an *I*, both ever-changing and the same. This Time lived as subject necessarily implies space, and is the pure intuition or *I* which is the catalytic energy or basis of all human knowledge. At this level of knowledge phenomena and noumena are fused into instants which are both time and not-time, and which are in fact the making of the timeless through Time. So that life, instead of being pure phenomenalism or pure materialism, is in fact a metaphysical activity in the course of which forms composing the world of mind make possible the conceptualization of the sensible world and its apprehension as pure ideas, that is to say their transformation into knowledge more and more in conformity with pure reason. This is the point where the Christian notion of redeeming the time through Time rejoins the Hegelian notion of transforming the real into the rational and matter into spirit, as well as the Kantian notion that the ideas of pure reason make it possible to shape and to organize perceptions and the concepts of practical reason into true knowledge.

There are two main types of knowledge—empirical knowledge, based on the understanding and the senses, and intuitive or imaginative knowledge which includes aesthetics and religion. Neither is objective, that is to say a mechanical recording of perceptions. This being said, the repudiation of the notion of objectivity is not to be taken as applied to the normal objectifying functions of the imagination and of the understanding, and not as a declaration of faith in pure subjectivism—Cartesian, Berkeleyan or otherwise. The repudiation of so-called scientific objectivity is merely a defence of the shaping activities of reason, and reason itself requires the separate and distinct existence of the objects and phenomena which it represents to itself and which are vital to its functioning and existence. In fact, reason exists and works because things and phenomena exist in themselves, and one is no more possible without the other than finite is possible without the infinite. Reason is the pure freedom of the phenomenal world, but it can only be so if there is a phenomenal world. That is what Kant meant when, in the *Critique of Pure Reason*, he said : 'The simple but empirically determined consciousness of my own existence proves the existence of objects in space and out of myself.' So much for Descartes' famous *cogito*, and even more arguable *ergo*, which makes of a purely subjective notion the basis of existence. God could perhaps use the two predicates of this saying, joined by the word 'and'—though one of them would be quite enough; but a finite being can only think something, and before thinking he has to be. Descartes' subjectivism as the basis of a theory of knowledge rejoins both Berkeley and Hume, and is unacceptable. It is evident that Thomistic realism has more to offer to modern thinking about knowledge than any form of subjectivism or purely mechanical materialism.

It is imaginative knowledge that, in spite of humanists, is the ultimate basis of ethics; for there is in the last resort no other basis to the commandment 'Thou shalt not kill' but a transcendental one. In the end true knowledge, including empirical knowledge, depends upon intuitive and imaginative knowledge. Even the scientist, who in his laboratory observes the evolutions of viruses and molecules, does so with projects and hypotheses in his mind, and therefore he fits his observations within a pattern which is part of a journey towards a truth which he hopes to discover, or which he has already glimpsed. He may even, in some strange cases, be so intent upon it or so obsessed by it that he may overstress or understress what he has observed. This last remark is made only in order to emphasize another aspect of the fact that empirical knowledge is never purely mechanical or objective knowledge, for although it rests upon the capacity of the understanding for conceptualizing empirical and perceptual data, there always enter into this operation both judging and patterning which involve intuitive thought and *a priori* synthetic knowledge. As Kant put it in the *Critique of Pure Reason*: 'The researchers of natural science had their revelation. They understood that reason only sees what it itself produces according to its own plans, and that it must take the lead with the principles which determine its judgment according to immutable laws, and it must also oblige nature to answer its questions and not to allow itself to be led on a leash by nature.'

Intuitive or pure knowledge is primarily concerned with the being of things apprehended through their appearing or representation, and with the wholeness of being to which these things belong. This form of knowledge, concerned with the being of things, that is to say with the being of being, is metaphysical or ontological knowledge, a type of knowledge which is at this moment practically ignored, or in many cases rejected by a form of pseudo-scientism which professes respect for reason and yet maims and diminishes it to such an extent that it considerably impoverishes human life and dangerously stunts its growth. Just as, at certain times in the past, the Church shackled some aspects of reason and claimed to be the only qualified mediator between the mysteries of the universe and man's deep longings and dreams, in our time the upholders of scientism— and there are millions of them—shackle and maim reason by seeking to reduce it to a cognitive and sense-perceiving instrument, thus fostering the strange mixture of attitudes which afflicts our purposeless world—sensualism and intellectualism.

We are living in an age of pure intellectual acrobatics which pass for imagination, of effervescence and continuous agitation in order to avoid reflection about and confrontation with the true human situation, and above all in an age of generalized indifference to human suffering because life is without roots, without past or finality except that which some scientists seek to discover or to anticipate in their laboratories or on the moon. In our science-obsessed age everything becomes laboratory work. Men experiment with love, sex, violence, human suffering, and to experiment is what matters. The guinea pigs—human beings—do not matter as long as experimental or statistical observations can be made and computerized, and results churned out. Tomorrow is no more important than yesterday; only today matters, and today is lived under the sign of a pseudo-rationality which is a denial of reason, since it denies its oneness. We are much concerned with knowledge in pre-digested forms which satisfy the craving for a veneer of learning, just as doggerel and uncontrolled daubings of paint on canvas satisfy the desire to be looked upon as an artist. We do not care at all, or very little, about real knowledge, real art, the true meanings of life or the ways of knowing, because these searches would compel us to leave the safe banister of pure empiricism and the surface phenomenalism to which we cling, and to face up to the problem of transcendental or pure knowledge. Of course mention of the word 'transcendental' is, in certain quarters, enough to raise murmurs about the meaninglessness of a concept which indeed can neither be proved nor disproved. So be it; every man is entitled to his opinions and beliefs, yet this is not an attitude which is resorted to by serious thinkers, even though they may be inclined to the view that it is not fruitful to examine such concepts at this moment, and that they may do more useful work by clearing up the linguistic obscurities and confusions which necessarily produce confused thinking, which has disastrous results upon life itself. This is a tenable and valuable attitude which I respect, particularly when it belongs to men of truly creative abilities and mental stature, but which I find unacceptable when it is used as a basis for dogmatism and narrow-mindedness by men who are scared of what they cannot guess or understand, seeking comfort for their limitations by having as many supporters as possible.

This being said, it seems to me that the very subdued definition of transcendental knowledge offered by Kant in *The Critique of Pure Reason* is such that it should raise the hackles only of those who shudder at the very mention of the words 'metaphysical', 'transcendental' or 'ontological'. He says: 'I call transcendental every knowledge which in general deals not with objects but with the way of knowing objects in as far as this mode of knowing is *a priori* possible.' The problem is not to examine the nature of being—something which cannot be done by a being which is part of it—but to determine the essence of transcendental truth which, as Kant says, 'precedes every empirical truth and makes it possible'. This explains both the impossibility of objectivity and the limitations of empiricism, if it is not mediated by pure reason. Empirical knowledge is knowledge of things, of nature, of man as individual and social being, but it does not deal with man as part of being, and this being is what unites men, what finds expression in their art, in their religion and in their higher mental speculations, which are as much part of his make-up and dynamism as his curiosity about and investigations of the natural laws that govern his life. The attempt to probe the relationship between man and being takes place in the domain of the imagination which connects the real, the physical, with the essential, and thus produces metaphysical knowledge which is as much part of the whole man as empirical knowledge. The problem of metaphysical knowledge which lies at the heart of Kant's *Critique of Pure Reason* is of vital importance to our age obnubilated by science, and therefore inclined to nurse the strange belief that the mind is an ever newly minted *tabula rasa*, ready to receive each perception or information as if it were the first one it had ever received. Those who do that ignore the fact that as Kant said in *The Critique of Pure Reason*, 'Whatever the ways or the means by which knowledge relates to objects, the mode by which it relates immediately to them is that thought always reaches them through the mediation of intuition.'

The point is that an object or a sensation never surges, in isolation and perfectly new, in front of the mind which is going to apprehend it. The mind is not only orientated, but it possesses already a kind of vague outline or representation, and also an image of the structural position of the objects or sensation that it perceives. The relation between mind and object can be direct, that is to say it can be an intuitive apprehension of the wholeness of the object, or it can be a relation that involves the various qualities and attributes of the object and their relationship to those of other objects. In this case, the relationship between object and mind is established through the understanding and is conceptual. Still, whatever the type of relation between mind and object, intuition is in different ways at the basis of these two types of knowledge, and this intuition, which plays a part in empirical knowledge as well as being the basis of speculative knowledge, is as impossible to quantify and qualify as the massless protons whose as yet undefinable position is the basis of Heisenberg's principle of indeterminacy. In speculative knowledge intuition creates its own object, which is not a representation or a concept of the object but an idea or essentialized image of human reality, the true worth of which depends on the depth and range of human truth which it embraces, something which consequently depends on the genius of the intuiting subject.

The intuition or the imagination attempts to render being apparent as part of finite knowledge. The poet, for instance, makes being apparent in the poem, which, in some ways, is not strictly speaking an object but a duration, a manifestation of being, itself born from the complex fusion of the poet's intuition with the emotions and reflexions caused by or connected with a situation, an event or a moment in time. An object is both a phenomenon and a thing in itself, which can only be known in as far as it manifests itself as phenomenon. There are therefore definite limitations to imaginative knowledge which pertain on the one hand to its finitude, and on the other to the fact that imagination cannot operate without the understanding's capacity to supply words and materials for representations and images. Kant's view is that 'our knowledge derives from two fundamental sources; the first is the capacity to receive representations (receptivity of impressions), the second that of knowing an object through these representations (spontaneity of concepts).' These two aspects of knowing are both equally important, at least in appearance, for one must not forget that even the objects perceived by the senses are structured by the forms of pure reason and that therefore the notion of a purely empirical knowledge unrelated to this aspect of reason is a meaningless notion. Facts can be made to yield different values and conclusions according to the hypothesis that presides over their selection. They acquire the meaning of the project they belong to, and new projects will bring out other qualities and other facets hitherto unnoticed. That is why in life one can never say that one has reached the final, ultimate solution of a given problem and there will not be any other. It is always a matter of time, and consequently of human imagination which is the individuating and ever-creating mediator between time and eternity. The use of the word 'eternity', which here means Being, might no doubt cause some impatience among those who find it a concept impossible to define, and who are therefore not prepared to accept any discussion involving such concepts. The problem is admittedly difficult, and yet it seems to me that no one has dealt with it better than Kant with his definition of *a priori* synthetic knowledge as pure thought or pure intuition and 'time as the *a priori* formal condition of all phenomena in general', time being thus the basis of transcendence.

The whole problem seems to rest on the question of whether it is possible for a contingent, finite being to have glimmers or partial apprehensions of being and of a type of knowledge which is pre-conceptual and which is therefore born from a direct relationship of the essence of being as pure thought with the transcendental essence of which it is an emanation. The fact that the individual is contingent upon or an emanation of transcendence, or possesses at any rate something transcendental, in the sense that its noumenal aspect cannot be encompassed by practical reason, must posit certain essential affinities between the two which make possible an apprehension of reality not through reflex concepts but as pure ideas as projections of reality. These ideas are part of the mind which recognizes them as inherent to its structures and therefore as part of its being. Based on pure thought, an emanation of the whole, intuition or imagination produces a form of knowledge which is organic and part of the coherence of the whole and is an appearance or a form of objectification of being. The true work of art is just that, and the artist can only achieve this result not through conceptualizations alien to art, but through states of receptivity and annihilation of the reflexive self, which make possible the emergence of being, and that takes place not at random but, as Kant says in the *Critique of Pure Reason*, according to predetermined affinities: 'We find that our thought, in relation to the knowledge of its object, always implies something necessarily expected; in fact this object is considered as something opposed to knowledge and our thoughts are not determined by chance or arbitrariness, but *a priori* in a certain way.' This determination or schematization is part of our nature and part of the historical and geographical background to which we belong. Our mental structures carry the marks of the sensibility of our history, our time and the society which they express, and they are such that a Japanese painter is as likely to paint a Japanese painting in front of a Western landscape as a Western painter is to paint a Western painting in front of a Japanese landscape.

The belief in objectivity is the stock-in-trade notion of the politicians and of the practitioners of pseudo-scientific methods in all aspects of life. They all ignore the fact that perceptions are not photographs or perfect copies of reality, but mental apprehensions of reality through the mind which is a natural schematizing, abstracting instrument. It can work on reality through the understanding, or it can, through the imagination, intuit time purely through images which are syntheses of mental representations of the senses or metaphors related to them. They are not contingent upon the being who thinks them; they are that very being becoming conscious of the timelessness of time; they are therefore part of the transcendental which cannot be excluded from life. The need to restore imagination and pure thought to their place in life has never been as urgent and vital as it is today, and in this domain I should like to give the last word to Kant who has convincingly explained their import-ance in the *Critique of Pure Reason* : 'Imagination is the capac-ity to intuit even without the presence of the object ... We have pure imagination as a basic faculty of the human soul, which is used *a priori* as the basis of all knowledge . . . Pure imagination is an indispensable function of the soul.'

Notes

CHAPTER 2

1. Jacques Monod, *Le Hasard et la Nécessité*, Le Seuil, Paris, 1970, p. 111.
2. *ibid.*, p. 117.
3. *ibid.*, p. 125.
4. *ibid.*, p. 142.
5. *ibid.*, p. 161.
6. J. D. Bernal, *The Origin of Life*, Weidenfeld & Nicolson, London, 1967, p. 4.
7. *ibid.*, p. 115.
8. *ibid.*, p. 130.
9. *ibid.*, p. 168.
10. *ibid.*, p. 195.
11. *ibid.*, p. 138.
12. *ibid.*, p. 139.
13. *ibid.*, p. 161.
14. J. Z. Young, *An Introduction to the Study of Man*, Oxford University Press, 1971, pp. 367–8.
15. *ibid.*, p. 369.
16. *ibid.*, p. 373.
17. *ibid.*, p. 372.
18. W. F. Hegel, *General Philosophy*, quoted in *Morceaux Choisis II*, Gallimard, Paris, pp. 318–9 (translation—J.C.).
19. A. N. Whitehead, *Science and the Modern World*, Macmillan, London, 1925, p. 26.
20. A. N. Whitehead, *Process and Reality*, Cambridge, 1929, p. 81.
21. Werner Heisenberg, *The Physicist's Conception of Nature*, Scientific Book Guild, Beaverbrook, 1962, pp. 48–9.
22. F. Bacon, quoted in Whitehead, *Science in the Modern World*, p. 58.
23. John Locke, 'Essay' in *Collected Works*, 1801, Book IV, Chapter VI, Section II.
24. *ibid.*, IV, VII, XI.

CHAPTER 3

1. Plato, *Timaeus*, ed. A. E. Taylor, Oxford, 1928.
2. Immanuel Kant, *Kritik der Reinen Vernunft*, Hartenstein, Leipzig, 1867, Vol. III, p. 16 (translation—J.C.).
3. Thomas Hobbes, *Leviathan*, Clarendon Press, Oxford, 1929, p. 41.
4. A. N. Whitehead, *Religion in the Making*, Cambridge, 1926, p. 32.
5. Whitehead, *Process and Reality*, p. 21.

CHAPTER 4

1. Simone Weil, *First and Last Notebooks*, Oxford University Press, 1970, p. 213.
2. Whitehead, *Religion in the Making*, p. 104.
3. Heisenberg, *op. cit.*, pp. 16–17.
4. René Descartes, *Oeuvres et Lettres*, ed. Pléiade, Gallimard, Paris, p. 191.
5. Jean-Paul Sartre, *L'Etre et le Néant*, Paris, 1943, p. 654.
6. Descartes, *op. cit.*, p. 188.
7. *ibid.*, p. 303.
8. H. Bergson, *Les Deux Sources de la Morale et de la Religion*, P.U.F., Paris, 1946, pp. 278–9.
9. Sartre, *op cit.*, p. 713.
10. Jean Rostand, *L'Homme*, Gallimard, Idées, Paris, pp. 173–4.
11. Jean Rostand, in *Monthly Information Bulletin* of the French Embassy in London, April 1971, pp. 12–13.
12. A. Einstein, from a lecture in Oxford, June 1933.
13. A. Einstein, *On the Method of Theoretical Physics*, Clarendon Press, Oxford, 1933, pp. 270, 276.

CHAPTER 5

1. Monod, *op. cit.*, p. 188.
2. *ibid.*, p. 189.
3. *ibid.*, p. 194.
4. *ibid.*, p. 192.

5. *ibid.*
6. A. N. Whitehead, *Religion in the Modern World*, p. 80.

CHAPTER 6

1. Sartre, *L'Etre et le Néant*, p. 713.

CHAPTER 7

1. Lord Zuckerman, in *Times Literary Supplement*, 12 November, 1971.

CHAPTER 8

1. Max Planck, in *International Forum*, 1931, No. 1.
2. A. Einstein, in a letter to Max Born, 7 September 1944.
3. Max Born, *Physics and Relativity*, London, 1956, p. 205.
4. A. Einstein, *The World as I See It*, London, 1935.

Select Bibliography

Alexander, S., *Space Time and Deity* (Dover, New York, 1927; Macmillan, London, 1966)

Augustine, St, *City of God*, ed. D. Knowles (Penguin, London and Baltimore, 1973)

    Confessions (Dutton, New York; Methuen, London, 1951)

Ayer, A. J., *Language, Truth, and Logic* (Gollancz, London; Dover, New York, 1946)

    The Problem of Knowledge (Macmillan, London; St Martins Press, New York, 1956)

    Logical Positivism (Allen and Unwin, London; Free Press, Glencoe, 1959)

    Philosophical Essays (St Martins Press, New York, 1954; Macmillan, London, 1963)

    The Foundation of Empirical Knowledge (Macmillan, London; St Martins Press, New York, 1964)

    Russell (Fontana, London, 1972)

    Russell And Moore (Harvard University Press, Cambridge, 1971)

Barth, Karl, *The Epistle to the Romans* (Oxford University Press, London and New York, 1968)

    God, Grace and Gospel (Oliver and Boyd, Edinburgh, 1959)

Berdyaev, N. A., *Space and Reality* (Bles, London, 1939)

Bergson, H., *Time and Free Will* (Allen and Unwin, London, 1910)

    Mind-Energy (Macmillan, London, 1920)

    Creative Evolution (Macmillan, London, 1911)

    An Introduction to Metaphysics (Macmillan, London, 1913)

    Matter and Memory (Swan Sonnenschein, 1911)

    The Two Sources of Morality and Religion (Macmillan, London, 1935)

Berkeley, G., *The Principles of Human Knowledge* (Macmillan, London and New York, 1945)

    Philosophical Writings, ed. Jessop (Nelson, Edinburgh, 1957; Nelson, Nashville, 1957)

Bernal, J. D., *The Origin of Life* (Weidenfeld and Nicolson, London, 1967; World, New York, 1967)

Bertocci, P., *The Person God Is* (Allen and Unwin, London, 1961; Humanities Press, New York, 1970)

Blanshard, *Reason and Goodness* (Allen and Unwin, London, 1961; Humanities Press, New York, 1961)

Boethius, *The Consolation of Philosophy* (Centaur Press, London, 1963; Bobbs-Merrill, Indianapolis, 1962)

Born, Max, *Physics and Relativity* (London, 1956)

Bouquet, A. C., *Hinduism* (Hutchinson, London and New York, 1966)

 Comparative Religions (Penguin, London and Baltimore, 1969)

Bradley, F. H., *Appearance and Reality* (Oxford University Press, London and New York, 1969)

Brett-Evans, P., *Masters of the Twentieth Century—Marx, Nietzsche, Freud* (Prentice-Hall, New Jersey, 1968)

Buber, Martin, *Between Man and Man* (Collins, London, 1960; Macmillan, New York, 1965)

Bultmann, Rudolph, *Primitive Christianity in its Contemporary Setting* (World, New York, 1956; Collins, London, 1960)

Collingwood, R. G., *The Principles of Art* (Oxford University Press, London and New York, 1950)

 The Idea of Nature (Oxford University Press, London and New York, 1949)

 The Idea of History (Oxford University Press, London and New York, 1949)

 Essays in the Philosophy of History (University of Texas Press, 1965; McGraw Hill, New York, 1966)

 Essays on Metaphysics (Oxford University Press, London and New York, 1940)

 Religion and Philosophy (Macmillan, London and New York, 1926)

Copleston, F. C., *Aquinas* (Penguin, London and Baltimore, 1970)

 A History of Philosophy (Burns and Oates, London, 1952–1966; Doubleday, New York, 1967)

Croce, Benedetto, *Aesthetics* (Peter Owen, London, 1953; Farrar, Straus, Giraux, New York, 1956)

Danto, A. C., *What Philosophy Is: A Guide to the Elements* (Penguin, London, 1971; Harper and Row, New York, 1971)

Descartes, R., *Oeuvres et Lettres* and *Discours de la Méthode* (Gallimard, Paris)

Einstein, A., *On the Method of Theoretical Physics* (Clarendon Press, Oxford, London and New York, 1933)

Ewing, A. C., *Non-linguistic Philosophy* (Allen and Unwin, London, 1968; Humanities Press, New York, 1968)

Farrer, A., *Freedom of the Will* (Humanities Press, New York, 1958; Black, London, 1963)

Findlay, J. N., *Hegel, a Re-examination* (Allen and Unwin, London, 1958; Humanities Press, New York, 1964)

Flew, A., *An Introduction to Western Philosophy* (Thames and Hudson, London, 1971; Bobbs-Merrill, Indianapolis, 1971)

    God and Philosophy (Hutchinson, London, 1966; Harcourt Brace, New York, 1966)

Foucault, M., *Les Mots et les Choses* (Gallimard, Paris, 1966)

Franklin, R. L., *Freedom and Determinism* (Routledge and Kegan Paul, London, 1968; Humanities Press, New York, 1968)

Frazer, J. G., *The Golden Bough* (Macmillan, London and New York, 1936)

Freud, Sigmund, *The Future of an Illusion* (Hogarth Press, London, 1962; Doubleday, New York, 1964)

    Totem and Taboo (Routledge and Kegan Paul, London, 1950; Norton, New York, 1952)

    The Interpretation of Dreams (Allen and Unwin, London, 1955; Avon, New York, 1967)

    Psychopathology of Everyday Life (Penguin, London and Baltimore, 1960)

    Civilization and its Discontents (Norton, New York, 1962; Hogarth Press, London, 1963)

    Leonardo da Vinci (Routledge and Kegan Paul, London, 1948, Random House, New York, 1966)

Fromm, Erich, *The Art of Loving* (Harper and Row, New York, 1956; Allen and Unwin, London, 1957)

    May Man Prevail (Doubleday, New York, 1961; Allen and Unwin, London, 1962)

    Man's Concept of Man (Ungar, New York, 1961)

Hampshire, Stuart, *Spinoza* (Faber and Faber, London, 1956; Barnes and Noble, New York, 1961)

    Thought and Action (Chatto and Windus, London, 1959; Viking Press, New York, 1960)

    Freedom and the Individual (Chatto and Windus, London, 1965; Harper and Row, New York, 1965)

Hegel, G. F., *Phenomenology of the Mind* (Macmillan, London and New York, 1931)

Esthétique de la peinture figurative (Hermann, Paris, 1964)
The Philosophy of History (Walley, New York)
The Philosophy of Rights (Oxford University Press, London and New York, 1971)
Hegel's 'Philosophy of Mind', ed. W. Wallace and A. V. Miller (Oxford University Press, London and New York, 1971)
Morceaux Choisis (Gallimard, Paris)

Heidegger, Martin, *Being and Time* (SCM, London, 1962; Harper and Row, New York, 1962)
    Existence and Being (Vision Press, London, 1949; Regnery, Chicago, 1950)
    The Question of Being (Twayne, New York, 1958; Vision Press, London, 1959)
    What Is Philosophy? (Columbia University Press, 1956; Vision Press, London, 1963)
    Kant et le Problème de la Métaphysique (Gallimard, Paris, 1953)

Heisenberg, W., *Physics and Philosophy* (Allen and Unwin, London, 1959; Humanities Press, New York, 1963)

Husserl, Edmund, *Ideas* (Macmillan, New York, 1962; Allen and Unwin, London, 1967)
    Cartesian Meditations (Nighoff, The Hague, 1960; Humanities Press, New York, 1960)

Jaspers, Karl, *Man in the Modern Age* (Routledge and Kegan Paul, London, 1951; Doubleday, New York, 1957)
    Tragedy is not Enough (Gollancz, London, 1953; Shoe String, Hamden, Conn., 1969)
    Three Essays (Harcourt-Brace, New York, 1964; Routledge and Kegan Paul, London, 1965)

Jung, Carl, *Psychology and Religion* (Yale University Press, 1938)
    The Undiscovered Self (Routledge and Kegan Paul, London, 1958; Atlantic Monthly Press, Boston, 1959)

Kant, Immanuel, *Prolegomena* (Manchester University Press, 1953; Barnes and Noble, New York, 1953)
    Critique of Pure Reason, ed. N. Kemp-Smith (Cedric Chivers, Bath, 1923; St Martins Press, New York, 1929)
    Critique of Practical Reason, trans. T. K. Abbott (Longmans, London, 1929; Bobbs-Merrill, Indianapolis, 1956)

Kaufmann, W., *Existentialism from Dostoevsky to Sartre* (Meridian Books, New York, 1956)
    A Critique of Religion and Philosophy (Faber and Faber, London, 1959)

The Owl and the Nightingale (Doubleday, New York, 1946; Faber and Faber, London, 1960)

Nietzsche, Philosopher, Psychologist, Antichrist (Princeton University Press, 3rd edition, 1969)

Hegel: Reinterpretations (Weidenfeld and Nicolson, London, 1966; Doubleday, New York, no date)

Kierkegaard, Sören, *The Journals* (Oxford University Press, London and New York, 1938)

The Concept of Dread (Oxford University Press, London and New York, 1957)

The Concept of Irony (Collins, London, 1956; Indiana University Press, 1968)

Either/or, A Fragment of Life (Princeton University Press, 1972)

Fear and Trembling (Oxford University Press, London and New York, 1954)

The Sickness Unto Death (London, 1946; Doubleday, New York, 1954)

Körner, S., *Kant* (Penguin, London and Baltimore, 1969, 2nd edition)

What Is Philosophy? (Penguin, London and Baltimore, 1969)

Leibniz, G. W., von, *Philosophical Writings* (Everyman, Dent, London, 1934; Everyman, Dutton, New York, 1934)

Discourses on Metaphysics (Manchester University Press, 1953; Open Court, La Salle, Ill., 1953)

Correspondence with Clarke (Manchester University Press, 1956)

Monadology (Oxford University Press, London and New York, 1898)

Levi-Strauss, C., *Les Structures Elémentaires de la Parenté* (Presses Universitaires de France, Paris, 1949)

Tristes Tropiques (Plon, Paris, 1955)

Anthropologie Structurale (Plon, Paris, 1959)

Totemism (Beacon Press, London and Boston, 1963)

The Savage Mind (Weidenfeld and Nicolson, London, 1966; University of Chicago Press, 1966)

Locke, John, *An Essay Concerning Human Understanding* (Collier-Macmillan, London and New York, 1965)

Löwith, Karl, *De Hegel à Nietzsche* (Gallimard, Paris, 1969)

Lowrie, Walter, *Kierkegaard* (Princeton University Press, 1938)

Luther, Martin, *What Luther Says*, anthology (Concordia, 1959)

MacMurray, John, *The Form of the Personal* (Harper and Row, New York, 1953–54; Faber and Faber, London, 1961)

Reason and Emotion (Faber and Faber, London, 1935; Barnes and Noble, New York, 1962)

The Structure of Religious Experience (Faber and Faber, London, 1939; Archon, Hamden, Conn., 1971)

Freedom in the Modern World (Faber and Faber, London, 1932; Humanities Press, New York, 1932)

Malinowski, Bronislav, *Freedom and Civilization* (Allen and Unwin, London, 1947; Indiana University Press, 1960)

Marcel, Gabriel, *The Mystery of Being*, 2 vols (Harvill Press, London, 1950–51; Regnery, Chicago, 1960)

Being and Having (A. and C. Black, London, 1948; Harper and Row, New York, 1948)

The Philosophy of Existence (Harvill Press, London, 1948; Books for Libraries, Freeport, New York, 1949)

Homo Viator (Aubier, Paris, 1947; Harper and Row, no date)

Maritain, Jacques, *Art and Poetry* (Kennikat, Port Washington, New York, 1969)

Art and Scholasticism (Sheed and Ward, London; Books for Libraries, Freeport, New York, 1962)

The Range of Reason (Scribner, New York, 1952; Bles, London, 1953)

Creative Intuition (Princeton University Press, 1955)

Freedom and the Modern World (Sheed and Ward, London; Gordian Press, New York, 1971)

An Introduction to Philosophy (Sheed and Ward, London, 1930; and New York, 1956)

On the Philosophy of History (Bles, London, 1959; Scribner, New York, 1959)

Science and Wisdom (Bles, London, 1940; Scribner, New York, 1940)

Twilight of Civilization (Bles, London; Sheed and Ward, New York, 1943)

Redeeming the Time (Bles, London, 1943; Hillary, New York, 1943)

St Thomas Aquinas (Sheed and Ward, London and New York, 1931)

The Rights of Man and Natural Law (Bles, London, 1963; Gordian Press, New York, 1972)

The Scope of Demythologizing (SCA)

The Peasant of the Garonne (Chapman, London, 1968; Holt, Rinehart and Winston, New York, 1968)

Medawar, P., *The Art of the Soluble* (Methuen, London, 1967; Barnes and Noble, New York, 1967)

> *Induction and Intuition in Scientific Thought* (Methuen, London, 1969; American Philosophical Society, Philadelphia, 1969)

Merleau-Ponty, M., *Phénoménologie de la Perception* (Gallimard, Paris, 1945)

> *Signes* (Gallimard, Paris, 1960)
>
> *Eloge de la Philosophie* (Gallimard, Paris, 1953)
>
> *Le Visible et l'Invisible* (Gallimard, Paris, 1964)
>
> *Humanisme et Terreur* (Gallimard, Paris, 1947)
>
> *Sens et Non-sens* (Nagel, Paris, 1948)
>
> *La Structure du Comportement* (Presses Universitaires de France, Paris, 1942)

Monod, Jacques, *Le Hasard et la Nécessité* (Le Seuil, Paris, 1970)

Moore, G. E., *Principia Ethica* (Cambridge University Press, London and New York, 1960)

Mounier, Emmanuel, *Existentialist Philosophy* (Barrie and Rockcliff, London, 1945)

Murdoch, Iris, *Sartre* (Yale University Press, 1953; Fontana, London, 1967)

Nietzsche, Friedrich, *Beyond Good and Evil* (Random House, New York, 1966; Allen and Unwin, London, 1968)

> *The Birth of Tragedy* (Doubleday, New York, 1956)
>
> *Thus Spake Zarathustra* (Allen and Unwin, London, 1968)
>
> *Unpublished Letters* (Peter Owen, London)
>
> *The Twilight of the Gods* (Penguin, London and Baltimore, 1969)
>
> *Pages Mystiques* (Laffont, Paris, 1945)
>
> *The Will to Power*, ed. W. Kaufmann (Weidenfeld and Nicolson, London, 1968; Random House, New York, 1968)

Parkinson, C. H. R., *Logic and Reality in Leibnitz' Metaphysics* (Oxford University Press, London and New York, 1965)

Pascal, B., *Pensées* (Hachette, Paris)

Pears, David, *Wittgenstein* (Fontana, London, 1970; Viking Press, New York, 1970)

> *Freedom of the Will* (ed.), Macmillan, London, 1969

Pieper, J., *Leisure, The Basis of Culture* (Faber and Faber, London, 1952; New American Library, New York, 1964)

> *The End of Time* (Faber and Faber, London, 1954; Pantheon, New York, 1954)

Scholasticism (Faber and Faber, London, 1951; McGraw Hill, New York, 1964)

The Silence of St Thomas (Faber and Faber, London, 1957; Pantheon, New York, 1957)

Introduction to Thomas Aquinas (Faber and Faber, London, 1963; Pantheon, New York, 1963)

Plato, *Plato, the Man and His Work*, ed. A. E. Taylor (Methuen, London, 1926; Dial Press, New York, 1927)

Plato's Socratic Discourses (Dent, London, 1920)

Plato, ed. Burnet (Oxford University Press, London and New York, 1903–08)

Popper, K., *The Logic of Scientific Discovery* (Hutchinson, London, 1956; Basic Books, New York, 1959)

The Poverty of Historicism (Routledge and Kegan Paul, London, 1960; Harper and Row, New York, no date)

Conjectures and Refutations (Basic, New York, 1962; Routledge and Kegan Paul, London, 1963)

The Open Society and Its Enemies (Routledge and Kegan Paul, London, 1962; Princeton University Press, 1966)

Raven, C. E., *National Religion and Christian Theology* (Cambridge University Press, London and New York, 1953)

Teilhard de Chardin (Collins, London, 1962; Harper and Row, New York, 1963)

Rhine, J. B., *The Reach of Mind* (Penguin, London, 1954; Morrow, New York, no date)

Russell, Bertrand, *History of Western Philosophy* (Simon and Shuster, New York, 1945; Allen and Unwin, London, 1953)

Human Knowledge (Allen and Unwin, London, 1948; Simon and Shuster, New York, 1948)

The Philosophy of Leibnitz (Allen and Unwin, London, 1937; Macmillan, New York, 1937)

Our Knowledge of the External World (Allen and Unwin, London, 1926; Humanities Press, New York, 1961)

Ruyssen, Théodore, *Kant* (Alcan, Paris, 1929)

Sartre, J.-P., *L'Etre et le Néant* (Gallimard, Paris, 1943)

L'Imaginaire (Gallimard, Paris, 1937)

L'Existentialisme est un Humanisme (Gallimard, Paris, 1960)

Critique de la Raison Dialectique (Gallimard, Paris, 1960)

Situations (Gallimard, Paris, 1942–65)

Schopenhauer, A., *The World as Will and Idea* (Routledge and Kegan Paul, London, 1907–9)

Spinoza, B., *Ethics and Corrections of the Understanding* (Dent, London)

Teilhard de Chardin, P., *The Phenomenon of Man* (Collins, London, 1960; Occidental, Washington, DC, 1968)
> *Le Milieu Divin* (French and Eur, New York, 1958; Collins, London, 1960)
> *Human Energy* (Collins, London, 1969; Harcourt-Brace, New York, 1971)
> *The Future of Man* (Collins, London, 1968; Harper and Row, New York, 1969)
> *Hymn of the Universe* (Collins, London, 1965; Harper and Row, New York, 1965)

Toulmin, Stephen, *Human Understanding*, vol. I (Clarendon Press, London, 1972; Princeton University Press, 1972)

Toynbee, A. J., *A Study of History* (Oxford University Press, London and New York, 1935–61)
> *The Present Experiment in Western Civilization* (Oxford University Press, London and New York, 1962)
> *Civilization on Trial* (Oxford University Press, London and New York, 1948)

Van Peursen, C. A., *Wittgenstein, Introduction to His Philosophy* (Faber and Faber, London, 1969; Dutton, New York, 1970)
> *Leibnitz* (Faber and Faber, London, 1969; Dutton, New York, 1970)

Vico, G., *The New Sciences* (Cornell University Press, 1968)

Waddington, C. H., *Behind Appearances* (Edinburgh University Press, 1970; MIT Press, Boston, 1970)

Wahl, Jean, *A Short History of Existentialism* (Greenwood, Westport, Conn., 1972)

Weil, Simone, *The Need for Roots* (Routledge and Kegan Paul, London, 1952; Harper and Row, New York, 1971)
> *Waiting on God* (Routledge and Kegan Paul, 1959; Harper and Row, New York, 1973)
> *Intimations of Christianity* (Routledge and Kegan Paul, London, 1957; Beacon, New York, 1958)
> *La Condition Ouvrière* (Paris, 1963)
> *La Connaissance Surnaturelle* (Paris, 1964)
> *Selected Essays 1934–43* (Oxford University Press, London and New York, 1962)
> *On Science, Necessity and the Love of God* (Oxford University Press, London and New York, 1968)

Whitehead, A. N., *Symbolism; Meaning and Effect* (Cambridge University Press, 1927; Putnam, New York, 1959)

    The Aims of Education (Benn, London, 1929; Macmillan, London and New York, 1959)

    Process and Reality (Cambridge University Press, 1927–8; Free Press, Glencoe, 1969)

    Adventures of Ideas (Macmillan, London and New York, 1933)

    Science and the Modern World (Macmillan, London, 1925; Free Press, Glencoe, 1926)

    Modes of Thought (Macmillan, Free Press, Glencoe, 1968)

Wittgenstein, L., *Tractatus Logico-Philosophicus* (Routledge and Kegan Paul, London, 1962; Humanities Press, New York, 1963)

    Philosophical Investigations, ed. G. E. Anscome (Blackwell, Oxford, 1968; Barnes and Noble, New York, 1969, 2nd edition)

    Wittgenstein, ed. Cyril Barrett (Blackwell, Oxford, 1970; University of California Press, 1967)

    Wittgenstein's Notebooks (Oxford University Press, London and New York, 1970)

Wollheim, R., *F. H. Bradley* (Penguin, London and Baltimore, 1969)

Young, J. Z., *An Introduction to the Study of Man* (Oxford University Press, London and New York, 1971)

Index

absolute, the, 16, 85, 87, 90; man's longing for, 26, 61; *see also* Being, God

absurd, idea of the, 65

actualization: of Being through being, 13, 44–6, 49, 57, 71, 72; of virtualities, 19, 29, 56, 66, 67; purpose of Being, to reach self-knowledge through, 68, 87, 119, 127; of God's will, 80

Aeschylus, 107, 113

aesthetics, 102, 105, 109; implied by religion and myth, 120; included in intuitive knowledge, 140

Anaximander, 60, 91, 94

anti-intellectualism, 127–8

anti-rationalism, 127

Aquinas, St Thomas, 53, 61, 108, 141; and philosophy of Aristotle, 99, 109

Aristotle: on essence or form, 30, 45; Aquinas and, 99, 109; on poetry, 110

art: Nietzsche on, 97, 100; transcendence of the subjective in modern, 98, 101, 125, 128; not interchangeable with religion nor a basis for morality, 102; truth of, 110; essentially rational, 111, 133

artist, task of, 40–1

atheism, 12; of Sartre, 62, 63; and science, 121

Augustine, St, 41, 45; synthesized Greek thought and Judaic existentialism, 60–1; on evil, 82; mentioned, 23, 90, 122

Bacon, Francis, 43, 99, 134
Baudelaire, Charles, 70, 106, 111, 125

becoming, 15, 36, 37–8, 43, 44, 96; Being as, 56, 71, 81, 87; purpose of Being to reach absolute self-knowledge through, 68, 87, 119, 127

behaviourism, 130, 134

Being, or God, 15, 36, 37, 38, 62; rationality of, 25–46, 111; society, religion and, 47–53; creation as separation of non-being from, 49, 55, 56–7, 66, 72; why is it, what is it? 54–69; is creativity, 54–6, 90, 126; is becoming, 56, 71, 81, 87; is both transcendent and immanent, 56, 66, 127; resolution of opposites in, 83, 126; will-to-appearance of (Plato), 122; *see also* absolute, actualization, God

belief: knowledge and, 90, 96, 98, 99; absence of a unifying, 120; in the spirit, 123

Bergson, Henri, 62, 120n; 'élan vital' of, 38–9, 122, 128; mentioned, 53, 123, 124, 127

Berkeley, George, 41, 141

Bernal, J. D., 32–4

Bernard, Claude, 136

Bohr, Niels, 57

Born, Max, on Einstein, 64, 136

Bradley, F. H., 127

British Association, clergy and, 121

Buddha, 107

categorical imperative, of Kant, 22, 78, 84, 133

chance, 17–24, 71, 101; as metaphysical and as operational concept, 9; use of term, 29–30; apparent interplay between determinism and, 67–8